PRAISE FOR *OPTIMISFITS*

Ben Courson is a vital voice for this generation. He discovers hidden truths in God's Word and communicates them in a refreshing way. *Optimisfits* will give you a new perspective on God…and on your own life.

Rich Wilkerson Jr., reality TV star of *Rich In Faith*,
author, and senior pastor of Vous Church

Once you have finished reading this book you'll know what it means to have authentic hope! Ben gives you a new way of thinking and tools for getting over the obstacles that are holding you back. And he does it with complete honesty and total transparency. If you aren't sure what God is asking of you, where you fit in, or like you are unqualified to live a life of real optimism, then *Optimisfits* is the perfect book for you!

Madeline Carroll, star of *Grey's Anatomy*,
I Can Only Imagine, and *Lost*

Optimisfits is goofy, funny, profound, and wise. It will reawaken that part of you that has forgotten how to enthusiastically embrace life in all its wonder. Hope is a message that people often don't know they need, but this book delivers it in all its unbridled splendor.

Tyson Spiess, star of *Tiny Houses*

Ben is adventurous, and his enthusiasm for life is contagious. He brings childlike wonder and honest faith together in such rare form. Check out *Optimisfits*!

Ryan Stevenson, Grammy nominated sing~~er~~ ~~~~iter
with #1 s~~~~ ~~~~rts

If you were to combine the positivity ~~o~~ ~~~~
Bolt, and the courage of Dietrich Bonh~~~~ ~~~~
his book *Optimisfits*. It is the perfect ext~~~~ ~~~~rson passionate about life, friends, the lost, and es~~~~ ~~~~out Jesus Christ. In every
chapter we learn about the importance of being who we really are, of failing

forward, and of laughing at fear. After reading this incredible book you will walk away motivated, challenged, and encouraged to take on life in a new and powerful way.

Stephen Christian, lead singer of Anberlin; over a million records sold

Ben has all the energy and style of a rapper or a DJ, and he brings a message of hope for all our daily struggles. He tears his chest open and spills his heart as his book shouts: "We cannot live without hope; the battle has already been won!" I've known Ben for a long time and always wished he would write a book. Now he has. You need to check it out!

Austin Carlile, lead singer of popular bands Of Mice and Men and Attack Attack!

A must-read! Ben is a living voice of hope for the future of our generation!

Meredith Foster, YouTube and Instagram celebrity

Ben is passionate about helping others find something to be passionate about. I love his message and his vision!

Kyle Singler, NBA basketball player

Ben Courson is a unique gift to this generation. From the moment I first heard him, I knew he would not leave the world as he found it. His unbridled joy, inquisitive nature, insatiable quest to learn, and depth of wisdom bely his years and make him one to watch. *Optimisfits* is more than a book— it's a prophetic call to a new and better way of living.

Terry Crist, TV host of *Café Theology* and lead pastor of Hillsong Phoenix

My friend Ben lives the countercultural message he writes about in this book, and he will give you the clear and simple direction you need to unleash hope, faith, and optimism in your life as you become an Optimisfit!

Levi Lusko, bestselling author, TV and radio host, and senior pastor of Fresh Life

Ben's message is: Embrace who you are because it's exactly who Jesus made you to be. Optimsfits is a must for anyone struggling to find their identity and purpose!

William Daniels, professional soccer player

Optimisfits is a bold call to reject social norms and embrace your uniqueness in a world that promotes blind conformity. Ben knows what it means to live a life that is both realistic and fearless, full of faith and hope.

Taylor Kalupa, star of *Law & Order* and *The Fix*

The first time I heard Ben speak about hope, it wasn't from a stage or a pulpit. It was face to face, from his heart. I love his message, but what really makes me love him as a person is his willingness to open up from a place of pain and vulnerability. It's all here in this book—tried by fire and truly authentic. Open up your heart and get ready to be challenged, changed, and charged up by this book!

Matt Hammitt, two-time Grammy-nominated and Dove Award-winning lead singer of Sanctus Real

I love this attention-grabbing, thought-provoking page-turner of a book! You won't be able to put it down, and when you finish, you'll want to become part of the Optimisfit squad. Thank you, Ben, for writing this life-changing book.

Carolyn A. Brent, award-winning author and star of *Across All Ages*

Optimisfits is amazingly energetic, biblically optimistic, and always fun! Ben faces life with a buoyancy and confidence that comes from working through his own pain and darkness. Do yourself a favor and read this book—and then pass it along to someone you love.

Skip Heitzig, national TV and radio host, author, and senior pastor of Calvary Albuquerque

Ben is leading the charge to fearlessly and boldly take ground back from the enemy. Dive into this book and let truth wash over you and purpose be ignited in your heart once again.

Masey McLain, star of *Christine* and *I'm Not Ashamed*

Has life brought you to your knees? Do you struggle with finding a life worth living? Are you trapped in a limiting, debilitating, anti-inspiring box? Well, this book is an axe to chop your way out! Join Ben, me, and our squad of *Optimisfits* on the journey of a lifetime—dreaming big, living abundantly, and fulfilling your destiny!

Ebo Elder, pro boxing champion

Ben has the ability to transform your entire life in one sentence, and *Optimisfits* will change the way you think about everything. A must-read!

Cambria Joy, author and YouTube celebrity

I'm praying that many people will encounter the presence and peace of God through Ben's brilliant and quirky writing style. He is free to be who God made him to be, and I love the reminder to be an Optimisfit!

Todd Doxzon, former NFL quarterback
and senior pastor of Love Church

You will be blessed by Ben Courson's book, which is full of great stories, profound insights, and a huge dose of biblical optimism. You'll walk away from this book with HOPE!

Daniel Fusco, TV host, author, a
nd senior pastor of Crossroads

Ben writes in such a fun and winsome style that you can't help but get swept up in the enjoyment and enrichment of this book. You'll walk away full of encouragement, hope, and a deep desire to be an Optimisfit yourself.

Ben Malcolmson, bestselling author and special
assistant to Seattle Seahawks head coach Pete Carroll

We all need more life-changing optimism, and if you need a potent dose to drown out hopelessness, look no further than *Optimisfits*.

Chris Brown, nationally syndicated radio host

This book will be a huge encouragement to those who need it. I believe in Ben's message and love reading his stories.

Chelsea Crockett, actress, author, and YouTube celebrity

Ben is the "Hope Evangelist." You'll find yourself writing in the margins of *Optimisfits* and returning to its pages often. I needed this message!

Perry Atkinson, founder and host of Dove Radio and TV

A relentless reminder that hope always has the last word. *Optimisfits* is engaging, insightful, and bursting with life. This is a message the emerging generation needs to hear. Ben's words will blow through the ashes of your fear and ignite your soul in hope.

Dominic Done, author of *When Faith Fails* and senior pastor of A Jesus Church

I've seen firsthand what happens when Ben speaks to crowds and how desperately this generation needs hope in their lives. Optmisfits will have a much-needed impact!

Ryan Ries, radio host and founder of the Whosoevers Movement

Ben has done more than write these pages. He has lived them. I've never met anyone more contagiously hopeful. This book set my misfit heart on fire with the hope of Jesus. It is a masterpiece! Read it at your own risk.

Austin French, *Rising Star* finalist and Billboard-charting singer

IGNITING A FIERCE REBELLION

AGAINST HOPELESSNESS

BEN COURSON

HARVEST HOUSE PUBLISHERS
EUGENE, OREGON

Optimisfits
Copyright © 2019 Ben Courson
Published by Harvest House Publishers
Eugene, Oregon 97408
www.harvesthousepublishers.com

ISBN 978-0-7369-7584-1 (pbk.)
ISBN 978-0-7369-7585-8 (eBook)

Library of Congress Cataloging-in-Publication Data is on file at the Library of Congress, Washington, DC.

Printed in the United States of America

19 20 21 22 23 24 25 26 27 / VP-SK / 10 9 8 7 6 5 4 3 2 1

Gen Z and Gen Y, millennials and centennials,
are now the most depressed generation on record.

This book is dedicated to all my Hope Generators
out there for knowing that fact…and defying it.

This book goes out to all you Optimisfits committed
to finding anything that isn't heaven on earth…and
utterly annihilating it.

CONTENTS

1

WHY BE WELL-ADJUSTED WHEN YOU CAN BE SAVAGE?

Being well-adjusted is seriously overrated.

I'm tired of knowing my place and toeing the party line.

Webster's dictionary defines misfit as "a person who is poorly adapted to a situation or environment."

Like it's a *bad* thing?

I think there is a lot to be said for the *poorly adapted*.

When you are trying to adapt to a culture that finds everything pretty much meaningless—who wants to adapt to that?

When you are trying to adapt to a culture that specializes in filters and computer tricks that make you look thinner and more gorgeous than you really are, and online posts that try to *impress* people rather than *impact* people—who wants to adapt to that?

When you are trying to adapt to a culture that is all about fulfilling the boring, conformist values of the "American Dream"—who wants to adapt to that?

And frankly, I'm not interested in trying to fit in with unthinking Christianity, made up of followers of an unquestioning vanilla-flavored brand of Churchianity, with all its tameness and sameness. Especially since the One who started it all was offering something more along the lines of a banana split with gummy bears and sprinkles on it.

So, when I am offered the opportunity to adapt to the System—in whatever form—then I will just politely decline.

Or maybe not so politely.

⦿⦿⦿⦿⦿

I'm proud to be a misfit.

Who really needs to "fit in" anyway? Sometimes it feels like we are moving ever closer to the world George Orwell envisioned in *1984*. A world where everyone is expected to conform, to take their proper place as a cog in the System, to just keep quiet and not upset the applecart, to do what is expected and unquestionably adapt, and to meekly submit to the subtle brainwashing that lulls us into complacency.

No. Just no.

I'm too busy nourishing my inner rebel, trying to keep alive to the things that really matter.

I'm saying no to being what the mighty J.D. Salinger's young Holden Caulfield called "a phony."

I refuse to believe that everybody's Instagram posts are telling it like it is. It is easy to slip into a comparison of our real life behind the scenes with the highlight reels that everyone else is posting. And then we begin to feel like our life is kind of boring in comparison.

It used to be that we tried to live up to the models we saw in magazines. Now we try to live up to our own Facebook profile.

So…if your life seems boring in comparison with other people's lives, maybe that means that it is time to change your life. Instead of focusing on a desperate attempt to get the attention of others, maybe it is time to just quit worrying about what other people think and decide to live your own adventure.

That's what I'm trying to do.

((((())))

No one ever accused me of being well-adjusted.

And I'm proud of that. I'm happy to be a misfit.

When I was a teenager I told my family and friends about some of the dreams I had for my life. Big dreams. Huge, hulking dreams.

I dreamed about having a show on TV and radio stations around the world. I imagined doing talk shows and radio interviews. I planned on writing a book that would be in bookstores everywhere.

Not because I needed the approval of my fellow featherless bipeds. I couldn't care less about that. But I had a vision about how God could use me to give hope to the world, especially to those who were struggling and confused and just plain tired of it all.

Maybe I was a little like Joseph, who couldn't keep his mouth shut about his coat of many colors. I was seventeen when I really began to grasp my dream, and I started telling people about it. They quickly let me know what they thought about all my dreaming. They told me to quit fantasizing and get serious. Some offered stern rebukes about recognizing my place. Or, more often, I just got a blank look from people who didn't know what to say, like the person who is dancing with you at a party but clearly wishes they were dancing with someone else. A few just smiled and humored me.

My dreams didn't fit with living an ordinary life.

Some tried to tell me that becoming a friendly neighborhood pastor would be the best way to accomplish what I dreamed about. But I knew that wasn't the answer. I couldn't see myself sitting in an air-conditioned office, answering emails and talking to parishioners whose main concern was that the music was too loud on Sunday.

That might be all right for some people, but it wasn't the dream God had given *me*. I tried that approach for a while, but it left me stressed and unhappy and unfulfilled.

So, I took ahold of my dream, believed in it, and did all the hard work I needed to do to make it come true. I worked hard. I sweated to the point of exhaustion. I ground it out. I failed, learned something from the failure, failed again, and then learned some more.

It was bitter before it was sweet.

And guess what? My dreams have come true, and what's more, I feel like I'm only at the beginning of the journey.

Because I didn't want to say yes to the well-adjusted and the average when I could be maladjusted and a *savage*!

I'm sure you have your own dreams. They probably look a lot different than mine. Which is good. It is in our uniqueness that we can make the most impact for God and others.

When you have the courage to pursue your own dream you are probably going to look like a misfit to the people around you.

But really, who cares?

Say no to conformity and expectations and ordinary-ness.

Nourish your inner rebel.

To do that you'll need some encouragement nourishment, and that's one of the things this book is all about.

When Henry Ford was first introduced to the famous inventor, Thomas Edison, it was as "the man trying to build a car that runs on gasoline." Upon hearing those words, Edison's face lit up and he slammed down his fist in excitement. "You've got it. A car that has its own power plant; that's a brilliant idea."

Up to that point, Ford had mostly met with ridicule and naysaying whenever he talked about his project. He'd come very close to giving up. But Edison's words ignited a new burst of confidence and became an important turning point in Ford's life.

"I thought I had a good idea, but I started to doubt myself," Ford once said. "Then came along one of the greatest minds that's ever lived and gave me his complete approval." This simple vote of confidence helped launch the automotive industry.

I hope this book is a vote of confidence for your dreams, so that when it comes to visioneering your future, you'll give everything…but up!

2

MISFITS OF THE WORLD, UNITE!

Sometimes it isn't easy to be a misfit.

If there were a Misfit Hall of Fame, then it would probably include such famous ones as Charlie Brown or Rudolph the Red-Nosed Reindeer. They were misfits who found their way despite everything that stood in their path.

For these misfits there is a certain kind of innocence and childlikeness that is both their strength...and their weakness.

They eventually triumph, but not before they miss kicking a few footballs and end up flat on their back, or detour to the land of misfit toys on their way to the North Pole.

You gotta love them.

Even if you don't want to *be* them.

But there is another kind of misfit—more antiestablishment and rebellious.

When you tell them to stay in their lane, to color within the lines, to toe the party line, or to do as they've been told—well, that just isn't happening.

They are the resistance.

They stand against the System.

Holden Caulfield in *The Catcher in the Rye*, the Beat Poets, Katniss Everdeen from *The Hunger Games*, and Jonas from *The Giver*. Real or fictional, these are people who refuse to bow to a System that is slowly killing people from the inside out.

Kierkegaard, Dostoyevsky, and G.K. Chesterton were also misfits, rebels against a cold and boring world, and against a cold and boring form of Christianity.

Why fit in?

All of these people—real and imaginary—are people who marched to the beat of a different drummer.

And if you listen carefully, maybe you can hear the rhythm of rebelliousness too.

(00000)

Let me tell you a story about a young preacher named Vincent.

He was an idealistic man of profound faith who wanted to serve others and share the gospel with them. He had been an art dealer but became disenchanted with that enterprise, so he decided to take a position as a missionary among the miners in a small Belgian mining town. A student of the New Testament, Vincent took its commands literally and chose to live a simple life, sharing the impoverished conditions of his small congregation. He shunned wealth and prestige.

He gave away most of his possessions and even became homeless for a time, sometimes sleeping in a haystack behind the home of the town baker.

Can you picture this in your mind's eye? Vincent would get up to preach before the congregation with bits of hay sticking to his clothes and the smell of bread wafting off him. The people loved him for his simple kindness and the passion with which he shared the gospel of Christ.

Vincent was committed to living like Jesus.

But the authorities of the missionary organization decided to pull their financial support from him. They thought it was unseemly for a preacher to live in the same kind of poverty as the people to whom he ministered. And his passionate faith embarrassed their dignified religiosity. Though he no longer had their support, Vincent tried to stay and serve his little flock, but his health soon began to fail.

And he felt like a failure.

In his spare time Vincent had begun to draw and paint, so now he decided to pursue a different dream—that of being an artist.

This disenfranchised, misfit, failure of a preacher became one of the most famous artists of modern times—Vincent van Gogh.

When, later in life, he painted his great masterpiece, "The Starry Night," Vincent envisioned a brilliant swirling night sky full of luminous stars above a small village filled with houses lit up against the darkness. But one of the buildings in the painting remained dark. There was no light coming from the church.

The church he had served faithfully had become a closed door for him.

If you, like me and like Vincent, have felt that religion has failed you, remember that you are not alone. The same thing happened to Jesus. The religious authorities of His day colluded with the Roman Empire to kill the young, idealistic Jew.

When you feel like your plans and passions have led to a dead end, remember that God has something bigger in store for you. The young missionary who preached to a tiny congregation became a painter whose artistry gave billions a glimpse of God's glory.

If your plans don't work out, maybe it's just because God has better ones for you.

If you can't see your way in the dark night of life, perhaps you need to look up at the swirling, shimmering stars and embrace God's hope.

◍◍◍

If you are a misfit you'll probably have to do battle with the temptation to become deeply pessimistic.

When you are different from the rest of the world, you see through its shallowness and falsity and fakery and phoniness. And pretty soon you might start to think that *everything* is shallow and false and fake and phony.

That can make you start to get cynical and skeptical and negative.

Note: There is a lot to be said for being realistic and asking good questions. I'm not asking anyone to become a simple-minded Pollyanna. Asking the right questions can save us from swallowing a pack of lies and deceptions.

But…

The danger of cynicism and skepticism is that they can make you a Grumpy Gus. They can stifle your sense of The Possible. They can turn you into a smug curmudgeon who stares out at the world from an ivory tower and judges everyone else to be ignorant, and therefore only worth ignoring.

And, honestly, it just takes a lot of the fun out of living.

When that happens, it is just another way that the System wins.

The only way to do battle with a debilitating *pessimism* is to embrace a fanatical *optimism*.

When you can be absurdly optimistic in the face of all the things that seem to be arrayed against you, you take away all their power to control your emotions, your decisions, and your sense of happiness.

When you see all the falseness of the world your vision no longer is opaque. You can see through it to a deeper and more satisfying dream-ality. You can get a perspective that isn't limited by this world, but sees a bigger picture.

In the face of everything that might try to bring us down, we can be optimists. Not people who approach life with an empty, plastic smile, but who make a choice to be happy in the face of life's pain. We can turn situations that are painful into *painfuel*, driving us onward to our destiny. We don't *react* to hardship, we *respond* to hardship. We are possessed of a kind of cheerful stoicism with a strength that moves heaven and earth.

That's how my friends and I are approaching life.

We embrace extremism. After all, there's no such thing as a moderate revolutionary. And Jesus didn't die to make us safe. He died to make us dangerous.

We are optimists.

We are misfits.

We are Optimisfits.

3

OF POOH BEAR, JESUS, AND DAVID FOSTER WALLACE...

Okay, let's get something out of the way right here.

The folks with the plastic smiles have always annoyed me. You know the type: all big grins and pretending that the sky is just about to start raining donuts of joy with all the sprinkles.

I know that sounds judgmental, but I just can't help myself. I'm trying to tell the truth in this book, and that's the truth.

Here's the way I see it...

When a person refuses to look honestly at the messy parts of life, the pretending that everything is okay all the time and plastering their face with a goofy grin that ignores all the very real pain, it drives me bonkers. When they come bounding into the room like Tigger, it just makes me feel even more like Eeyore. When they imply that they have some secret pass to the Land of Awesomeness and that I'm missing out on the great time they're having, I just want to say "no thanks." I can do without their kind of optimism if it means traveling with my eyes closed to the struggles of life.

I wish I could take hold of both sides of their face, look them in the eye, and say, "Really? You must be kidding me. Wake up!" The world isn't a place that rains jellybeans and Skittles.

Or.

Do they know something I don't know?

Or is it just that I think there is a more substantive kind of optimism available.

Maybe these smile-a-minute chaps are so busy with life's exclamation points that they can ignore the question marks. They probably think that a question mark is just an exclamation mark that got bent out of shape. But I can't ignore the questions…and I have a lot of them.

⬤⬤⬤⬤⬤

Religious optimists are the worst kind. I often require an aspirin after talking with them.

They often aren't really thinking for themselves. They just parrot a lot of nice little Christian phrases about how happy they are because "after all, brother, God is good all the time and all the time God is good." But I'm not convinced they really believe this. They're busy downplaying the pain of life instead of being really honest about the fact there is a darkness and sickness within us that is the very thing Jesus came into the world to heal. Kierkegaard called it the "sickness unto death." I don't think he'd have much patience with this fake cheeriness either—these Band-Aids slapped onto gaping wounds.

Marx argued that religion was the opiate of the people. And many churchgoers are unwittingly brainwashed into confirming his critique. They've drunk the Kool-Aid. You can see the evidence at the corner of their smiles.

This kind of approach doesn't seem to me to have much to do with real spirituality. This is just another form of Churchianity. Just another manifestation of religion.

No thanks.

There is a lot about life that is confusing and painful. Stuff that just doesn't make much sense to me. I am left with a whole bunch of questions:

Why does it seem like most of my relationships come with non-rechargeable batteries that eventually seem to drain out and die?

Why do I have to see suffering so close-up? Last week as I was driving somewhere with my buddy Cam, we watched as one of the cars in front of us hit a baby deer that was crossing the road. It got caught underneath the vehicle, tumbling and thumping along until it came careening out from underneath. The driver peeled away without batting an eye, fleeing the scene. We pulled off to the side of the road and watched as another driver got out of his car and dragged the (still living) deer's face across the pavement so that oncoming traffic could continue going nowhere fast. Why did I have to watch the fuzzy belly rise and fall as Cam put his hand on the little guy to ease his pain as death rattled in his throat? He kept gently stroking that soft fur until all the life had disappeared from the little fawn. This made me want to cry.

Why do I sometimes feel so sad that I can't cry?

Why did I get beat by chronic depression for ten years?

And why did I smile like everything was fine?

Why did David Foster Wallace, one of our greatest modern writers, kill himself? He was a brilliant writer and a brilliant thinker, but even he couldn't figure out how to survive. He once said that suicide was a lot like jumping out of a burning building. It's not that you're not afraid of falling; it's just that falling is the lesser of two terrors. I guess he took his own words to heart.

Why did my sister die?

The memory is etched like psychic acid on my brain. I remember being eight years old and sitting in my classroom thinking about precisely nothing when my next-door neighbor came into class and approached my teacher. It was a wintry day, and my neighbor's eyes were the same gray as the slushy snow outside the classroom window, the leftover kind you wish would just melt away already. As she walked me home, she wouldn't tell me why I was being taken out of school. I guessed that maybe my family was going to throw a surprise party for me. Instead, I felt something strange and heavy hanging in the air when I walked into the living room. The room was not as light as it should have been for that time of day, as though the lamps were struggling against the darkness and gloom. My family was all gathered around, looking confused as the tears formed in their eyes. My dad looked up and told me that my sister was in heaven now. She'd been in a car accident. She was only sixteen.

And so it goes.

This is what the world really looks like. It's not too difficult to become a pessimist.

◯◯◯◯

I refuse to become a pessimist. I don't want to be the guy who sees the glass completely empty or the guy who sees a cloud in every silver lining or the guy who can give you ten good reasons why you should be miserable.

Maybe part of the problem is that I'm a little bit jealous of the people who are always happy. Because once I was one of those people.

When I was young, I was a flaming optimist. I was always happy and upbeat. A veritable lump of sunshine. In high school I was voted student body president, won the homecoming crown, and was a star basketball player—one of the leading scorers in Orange County, California. I was living the dream. I'd sometimes have as many as 200 people at my house for Bible studies or to play a game of basketball in our pool. I would often go to the beach after school and join my friends at Disneyland on the weekends. I dated the homecoming queen.

Life was a party.

And then, in the middle of my senior year, my perfect world came crashing down around my ears. The truth about how harsh this world can be finally caught up with me. I found myself face-to-face with what Churchill called "the black dog of depression" and everything changed. I can't even tell you exactly what went wrong or what chain of events led me to this dark place.

My optimism circled the drain and disappeared down a dark hole of hopelessness.

I had lived many years with a carefully applied smile on the outside while I was dying on the inside. In fact, I really wanted to die. I toyed with the thought of suicide and about how I might most effectively accomplish such a task.

My faith in God began to vanish, and Christianity began to seem fake. I was beginning to awaken to the suspicion that I'd fallen for an effective sales pitch, but was now unsure about the product I'd invested in. Perhaps Jack Kerouac was right. Maybe God was just Pooh Bear; a helpful figment of my imagination which existed to make me feel better. I wondered.

When I got honest with my friends, I found that they were struggling in the same way I was. They didn't know how to integrate the dark thoughts and realizations about life into their day-to-day experiences. They couldn't make sense of the pain. And the form of faith they learned in church didn't offer much help either. So, they became angsty, cynical, hopeless, and sad. For them, as for me, the Hallmark-card, fortune-cookie adages offered by religion didn't cut it anymore. We couldn't live with such a denial of reality.

(((())))

I hated being so pessimistic, but I couldn't jump on the bandwagon of churchy optimism either. *Are these really the only two options?* I asked myself. *Being a gloomy agnostic or a simpleminded Christian?*

There has to be a third alternative, right? A way of looking at life that embraces authentic hope and ultimate meanings, while at the same time isn't afraid to be honest about the pain and confusion and misery that we sometimes experience in the course of living as a human being?

Well, I stumbled upon a third alternative.

It's what I refer to as being an *Optimisfit.*

What, you ask, is an Optimisfit? Well, as the name implies, it is someone who embraces his or her misfit identity and doesn't neatly fit inside the comfortable religious box…but who manages to hold on to a wildly optimistic view of life even in the face of all the darkness around us. The Optimisfit knows that life doesn't come with nice, neat right angles.

No, life is messy and wild.

And so are the Optimisfits.

In this book I am going to introduce you to the Squad—the people who share this Optimisfit life with me. We are all living life together as rebels against hopelessness.

We stand against the false narratives of cynicism and nihilism.

We stand against the kind of Christianity that makes life all about being careful, boring, safe, and conformist.

We love God, but we want to live in a different kind of way.

We want to rebel against both the culture of hopelessness…*and* against the culture of vanilla-flavored Churchianity.

That's how we roll…

4

THE OPTIMISFITS

So, who are the Optimisfits?

We Optimisfits embrace an adventurous lifestyle. We go on adventures with our Squad…and adventures with God. We aren't interested in working 40 hours a week for 40 years to retire on 40 percent of our income. There's nothing wrong with hard work, but you have to make room in your life for a little crazy adventure or two. We love to explore this magical planet God made. We hike the Matterhorn, we go four-wheeling in abandoned water parks, we explore the hidden waterfalls of Oahu, and we do handstands at the Eiffel Tower.

We embrace an adventurous life of the mind. We skateboard and we read Kierkegaard. We aren't afraid to explore the dark places of human existence with Kurt Vonnegut and Sylvia Plath. We read fantasy novels and remind ourselves that we already live in Narnia.

We live by nobody else's rules.

When someone tells us something is impossible, we see it as a dare rather than a declaration. If it is impossible, we do it anyway. If William Pitt the Younger could become the Prime Minister of England at age 24, then what holds us back from tackling anything in our path?

After all, we're too young to realize that certain things are impossible.

So we will do them anyway.

◯◯◯◯

Rather than seeing the glass as either half-full or half-empty, we just see the glass as *totally full*. We say with David, "My cup…runneth over."

(Miscellaneous random scientific insight: Technically the glass is totally full; one half is full of hydrogen and oxygen, and the other half is full of nitrogen and oxygen. David was onto something, eh?)

We don't wink at suffering. We don't act like pain isn't real. We just choose to face it and conquer it. We have nightmares. We have dreams. We can conquer our nightmares because of our dreams.

We are all about hope. We hate clichés about Christian joyfulness heard many a Sunday morning that frankly don't work. But neither are we timid about expressing how recklessly hopeful we are choosing to be. We share the certainty of Julian of Norwich: "All shall be well, and all shall be well, and all manner of things shall be well." That's a motto we can believe in.

We are antiestablishment. Rebels. Dreamers. We choose to live like Jesus. Like Him, if we are going to offend anyone it will be the religious people. We love them but we aren't going to cater to them. We aren't vanilla. We are extreme.

We are all about having fun. We believe that fun is what will change the world. And we want to change the world. Steve Jobs, the founder of Apple, once said, "The ones who are crazy enough to think they can change the world are the ones who do it." Yeah, we are a little crazy. Okay, maybe a lotta crazy. But it is misfits like us who can show people a different way to live.

⬭⬭⬭⬭

Why am I an Optimisfit?

I am fully confident that in the big book of my own story, when the last line is finally written, it will cast light backward into the darkest corners of the earlier chapters of my life. I don't have to understand everything now. But I'm not pretending that the darkness isn't real and that sometimes life isn't hard. The philosophy of the Optimisfit allows me to remain fantastically hopeful in the face of whatever life throws my way. It understands that such hope can be an act of fierce rebellion against the hopelessness of the world.

This isn't a journey I travel alone. My Squad is made up of a bunch of hope dealers, and there's no place like hope. They've given me a place of belonging.

I didn't always live so boldly. I wasn't always so wild. I wasn't always so enthusiastic about life. I used to feel like an outcast. I didn't feel like I fit in anywhere. I was without much purpose. I wandered alone.

And then I wandered into the arms of my fellow Optimisfits.

I hope you'll join me there...

5

GOD AND MY SQUAD

I used to be a loner.

For much of my life, particularly during my twenties, I didn't have a lot of friends. I told myself that I was just too busy to hang out. I was defined by the grind. I would hustle and sweat and work long hours. And I was miserable. But it took me a while to catch on to that fact.

I became my own best company. As long as I was burning the midnight oil I thought I was happy. Work meant more to me than friendships. My best buddies were those who'd written the books I loved—people like C.S. Lewis, G.K. Chesterton, Shakespeare, Kierkegaard, and George MacDonald. Problem was, they were all dead.

Frankly, this made for a rather one-sided conversation.

Then I discovered the power of Squad. The old-fashioned word is *community*, but I found myself surrounded by a group of people who *didn't* just commune—they dived into life with all the purpose of a sports team intent on winning.

It happened because God brought actual living human beings into my life. They pulled me out of my own head. They gave me something to think about beyond the unholy trinity of me, myself, and I…and the boring life the three of us led together. It was like going from womb to world, or caterpillar to butterfly. It was like messing about with Minions before taking flight on the Millennium Falcon. I took the jump from solitude to solidarity. With my Squad at my side I could live a better life. I went from loneliness to the joy of real friendship.

It is better to infiltrate than to isolate. If you want to go fast, go alone. If you want to go far, go together.

The way not to give up is to Squad up.

My friends and I are living a different kind of life with God. We are embracing a different kind of optimism. Not just wishful thinking, not just positive thinking, but *transcendent* thinking. We aim to transcend both the churchy optimism that is out in the weeds, as well as the atheistic pessimism that leaves everyone in the dumps, by acting with a fearless hopefulness. We refuse to let the world just happen to us. We happen to the world.

We are ridiculously hopeful and unapologetically rebellious. And we are in this adventure *together*.

Too many people die with their song still inside them. Too many people die in their twenties and are buried in their seventies. Too many people exist, but don't actually live. They breathe and perspire, but they are acting like not much more than a bag of bones and a carbon footprint. They are alone. And they despair.

Our generation tries to deal with this loneliness by popping pills to keep us cheerful, checking our iPhone every 20 seconds to see if we still matter, by trying to build our virtual kingdom in *World of Warcraft 25*, and by watching way too much television. Stephen King once said that it is not the great tragedies of life that make one suicidal, but that sometimes one just gets tired of watching afternoon television.

Here in America we consume more pills to ease our depression and anxiety (by three times) than the rest of world combined. Antidepressants are some of the fastest-selling prescribed medications in the United States. Suicide is one of the top-ten causes of death here in the land of broken hearts. We are a nation built on life, liberty, and the pursuit of happiness; but we are stressed, distressed, depressed, and in deep debt.

Earlier in this book I referred to my depression. It's been said that the scars you share become lighthouses for others. Maybe I can help you avoid some of the rocks that nearly shipwrecked me.

Depression is awful.

During my own long fight with despair I hated waking up in the morning to face another day. I was like Finnick in *Mockingjay*. I would drag myself out of nightmares every morning to find no relief in waking. My future stretched out before me as an infinite grayness, with nothing to look forward to that I could actually take any joy in. I knew God was walking alongside me in my shadowy valley, but somehow that didn't stop me from despairing of life whenever dawn rolled around.

To make things worse, I was a pastor.

As a pastor you are supposed to have your act together. You are supposed to be able to inspire others, but I couldn't even inspire myself. You are supposed to have the answers, but all I had was a growing list of questions. I was just so tired that all I wanted to do was lie down and sleep.

Here I was, the 18-year-old wunderkind. I was good at what I did. People said that they found my sermons wiser than my age would allow for. I was telling people how to find peace and joy with God, but inside I felt empty. The harder I tried, the more depressed I became.

I tried to act like the good churchy pastor, but I was really more interested in watching *Star Wars* again (for the eighty-seventh time) or shooting hoops than in hanging around people who were expecting me to be the somber, serious saint everyone expected me to be.

I started to quote from Ecclesiastes a lot in my talks. My life verse became, "Meaningless, meaningless. Everything is meaningless." I agreed with Herman Melville that Ecclesiastes was the truest book in the Bible. It summed up how I felt pretty neatly. And even on those mornings when I kept busy and felt a little more okay, I knew that by midafternoon the poisonous bank of mental fog would come rolling in.

And I thought about death. A lot.

Since many of the greatest people in history had struggled with this same battle that I was facing, I found a little bit of ironic encouragement in that. After all, the great prophet Elijah was almost suicidal in his despair. Job cursed the day he was born. Abraham Lincoln sometimes walked alone in the woods with a shotgun cradled in his arms, tempted to kill himself. Winston Churchill had to insist on a flat on the lower floor lest he decide on a whim to fling himself off the balcony. And Charles Spurgeon, the "Prince of Preachers," would descend into crippling depression every Sunday night after spitting out golden words that very morning.

If the great thinkers found life gloomy, who was I to argue?

My mind was as full of scorpions as Macbeth.

But then everything changed.

⦿⦿⦿

You might think I am going to tell you about some life-changing ecstatic religious experience, or how God appeared to me in bodily form to tell me everything was going to be okay, or that I won the lottery and now all my dreams could come true.

Nope.

It was nothing like that.

Instead, a Squad of Optimisfits invited me out of my loneliness and called me to quit all the existential navel-gazing.

Every person has a different story, and I'm not saying that everyone's depression will be lifted in the same way that mine was. Nor am I saying that it was a magical, overnight transformation. But I am saying that I had to get outside of my own head and start embracing my need for people in my life. Friends. A Squad of fellow travelers. Not just God, but people. I couldn't do life by myself, and when I realized that fact, things began to change.

These people taught me that I needed to stop being vanilla and boring and predictable. They told me to stop apologizing that I couldn't live up to other people's expectations for me. They showed me how to dance in defiance of the dark.

They taught me how to have fun.

Alone, life was a philosophical problem. With them, life was an adventure.

We decided that life was a splendid thing, and that we could suck all the marrow out of life, just like Thoreau said. We could put to rout all that was not life. A life of quiet desperation? Well, that was for chumps.

Instead we wanted to walk with the *living* God here in the land of the living. Walking with God is fun. He's the One who put the *fun* back in funeral. God and the Squad—that was the secret we'd found to happiness and meaning. We wanted to change the world, and we realized that changing the world would be the best kind of fun. And fun was the best way to change the world.

We'd skateboard and excitedly discuss the finer points of C.S. Lewis' *The Great Divorce*. We'd live crazy to show the world that hopelessness is not the only option for how to live. We'd be the alarm clock to awaken the soul of a country that has put its hopes to bed.

〇〇〇〇〇

Now that I have invited friends into my life, I can see so much more clearly. When C.S. Lewis was alone and bereaved after the death of his wife, he wisely wrote, "You can't see anything properly when your eyes are blurred with tears." So true. My Squad helped me see clearly again. They showed me that God doesn't want my life to be miserable. He wants my life to be memorable. We may sow in tears today, but we will reap in joy tomorrow.

If you are trying to go it alone, let me encourage you to find your own Squad. It doesn't happen overnight. It takes some risking, a lot of vulnerability, and putting your fear of being known aside. But you can find a better life when you pursue life with others.

Open up.

Squad up.

And embark on the *friendventure*.

6

FROTHY AND SCHLUMPED

Brighton is one of the members of my Squad.

You'd like him. Everybody does.

To be honest, he's just a tiny bit this side of crazy. He's been known to sneak into the offices of Palm Springs executives and decorate his arms with the little ink stamps they use for marking documents. These temporary tattoos are his way of showing that he isn't going to be brainwashed into conformity like Winston Smith in Orwell's *1984*. He's his own sort of marked man, using office supplies to announce his rebellion against the ordinary and expected.

Brighton has a feverish and single-minded dedication to having fun. There isn't anyone else like him in the known universe…and I suspect in the unknown universe as well. He's a Californian who dresses like some sort of dancer or white rapper. He pretty much dances everywhere he goes. Everything is background music for his life. It has been said that children have yet to learn that there is anything that isn't music. That's how it is for Brighton. There is always music in his head.

A lot of that music is EDM. Just in case you don't know, and to save you having to use your dictionary app, EDM is Electronic Dance Music. A couple of weeks ago he took me to an EDM concert. Brighton danced like a wild man. We lost ourselves for a while in the throb and hum of the music and the dazzling light show. The stage lights cast an icy blue over everything. The brilliant colors were the neon of my childhood and the white was like moonlight on snow. I was filled with ecstasy and wonder and my soul fell open to the effects of the sights and sounds.

The concert baptized my imagination, just like the book *Phantastes* did for C.S. Lewis.

Brighton reminds me that there is much more mystery to this world than I often notice.

Part of his skill set is what he can do on a skateboard. It makes your jaw drop. *Dude. How does he do that?* And he is smart, the recipient of a perfect 4.0 grade point average.

Brighton might be best described as *frothy*, which is one of his favorite words. That and *schlumped*.

Brighton has two speeds: dead stop and 97 miles per hour. He is either lazy as a sloth or he is bouncing on a trampoline, his veins bulging as he performs four backflips in a row while screaming something that sounds like "*boiiiii*."

In that crazy frothy head of his, Brighton hears the Muses sing.

When Brighton starts to wax lyrical, he talks about stuff like "the eye of the scorpion." I have no idea what that means. And you never know when he will lapse into gibberish, a language of his own creation that is about as intelligible as Klingon. For no particular reason he likes to call me Daryl.

His 4.0 notwithstanding, he talks like a stoner. As though all the dendrites in his brain are fried.

But his mental state has nothing to do with drugs. It is the result of being someone who just embraces all the joy of life with a childlike wonder. This is probably what makes him a great photographer—in fact, one of the most admired photographers in the known universe, and probably in the unknown universe as well. He is someone who lives with his eyes wide open, taking it all in, and then transforming ordinary things into something beautiful.

He loves to listen to electronic music artist Illenium as he works on his photos. He describes the music as being that of angels pouring honey down his ear. He edits turquoise and flame hues into his photos. The result is unbelievable. His twilight pictures capture the fire and garnet of the sunset, as if the night is on the edge of becoming and the day has not quite run out of things to say to itself. He makes clouds look like flamingo feathers and stars like exploding fireworks falling through the everlasting. They are like sapphires set against the inky dark of inter-stellar velvet. When he captures the night sky in his lens it looks like every twinkling star is God walking over one of the leaks in heaven's floorboards.

He loves to take photos of people's eyeballs, zooming in so close it looks like galaxies are melting in their irises. Everyone looks out from their eyeballs, but he looks *into* them.

He is kind of a mad genius.

And for all his artistry, he doesn't take any of his art that seriously. There is a reckless devil-may-care touch to his work that makes it irresistible. That changes the way you see the world.

Jesus said, "If you want to save your life, lose it." Perhaps the same prin-ciple can be applied to art. If you want to make serious art, take it less seriously. And if you want to live a serious life, take yourself less seriously.

⬡⬡⬡

The person who changed the world more than anyone else was a little bit like Brighton. Jesus was anointed with the oil of gladness above all His fellows. He was serious about His mission. He was serious about loving people. But He lived with a childlike, reckless wonder. No one loved life more than He did. He was the happiest person ever to live.

Jesus enjoyed the joy of being enjoyed by God.

"Just wait a minute," the cynic will reply. "Jesus said following Him was carrying a cross—an instrument of torture. So, walking with God isn't easy."

I reply that Jesus said His burden was light. He did all the heavy lifting on our behalf so that we don't need to carry a burden. If your walk with God is burdensome rather than light, you're doing it wrong.

So, what did He mean when He talked about carrying a cross?

Maybe a little history lesson would be helpful. When Jesus was about 11 years old, a misfit named Judas the Galilean raided the Roman armory just four miles from Jesus' hometown. In a swift and merciless response, the Romans crucified two thousand of the rebels along the roadside. Jesus would have walked along that road and seen those poor rebels hanging on crosses. Surely that memory would have etched itself on His brain like psychic acid. Carrying a cross meant that you were submitting to the Roman government as they executed you. It meant you turned the other cheek rather than fight back.

The Jews wanted to take up their swords against the Romans. Instead, Jesus told them to take up crosses. He told them to opt for peace rather than war. He said that instead of revenge, they should love their enemies.

Carrying a cross has nothing to do with living a miserable life in which we believe that God is opposed to everything we enjoy. Carrying a cross is an anti-violence message. It isn't about sacrificing your dreams or denying your pleasures.

Remember. At His right hand "are pleasures forevermore" (Psalm 16:11 ESV).

Fun, my friends, is fundamental.

7

PROBING THE WOUNDS

Many people succumb to the temptation of over-analyzing their own lives—of mentally rethinking all the mistakes and pains of the past. This tends to destroy an optimistic outlook faster than just about anything else.

I don't see much purpose in navel-gazing.

In 1881 James Garfield was elected the twentieth president of the United States. Six months later, this Civil-War hero was shot in the back by an assassin. The doctors were able to save his life, but for all their efforts they were not able to locate the bullet. Though he was recovering just fine, in those days doctors believed that it was essential to remove the bullet so that it wouldn't cause problems later. So they did more surgeries and probed all around, but still couldn't find it. They even tried a new electrical invention from Alexander Graham Bell that they hoped would locate it. That didn't prove successful either. Two months later President Garfield died—not from the original gunshot wound, but from the infection that came along with all the probing around.

Moral of that story: Sometimes it is better to leave things alone. If you're always probing around your hurts, your wounds, and your failures, you are never going to get well.

Our tribulations are never fatal, but our pessimistic probing into them just might kill us in the end.

UGLY PAUL AND MONSTER BARBIE

Paul, the great apostle to the Gentiles, lived in *beast* mode. He traveled to far-flung places, unlike Jesus, who rarely traveled beyond His home country. Following the vision God gave him of the Macedonian man, Paul followed in the footsteps of Alexander the Great, but he was undertaking a conquest for the Kingdom of God.

One area where Paul spent a great deal of time was Greece. The Greek culture wasn't immediately ready to hear the message, what with their pantheon of gods and goddesses and assorted semidivine beings. And what the Greeks valued above almost everything else…was beauty.

One of the reasons that Paul might not have been the most likely candidate for impacting the entire culture of Greece is that Paul was ugly.

You'll never dig up a Greek statue of an ugly person. Their sculptures idealized the human form. They made the gods look like ideal human beings and human beings look like gods. Masculinity in chiseled marble and femininity in perfect form. When the later Renaissance artists needed a guide to what the ideal human being should look like, they used the Greek models.

So, when Paul brought his message to Corinth (in Greece), the Corinthians found him to be a disappointment. Sure, his sentences were beautifully crafted and his logic careful and precise, the kind of thing they admired. But though his words were weighty, they found his bodily presence less than impressive.

We know that Paul was kind of ugly because of the description provided in a book called *The Acts of Paul and Thecla,* an apocryphal work that dates back to around AD 200. In it, the great apostle is described as "a man of little stature, thin-haired upon the head, crooked in the legs, of good state of body, with eyebrows meeting, and with nose somewhat hooked." He was, in short, a bald, bandy-legged little dude with a unibrow that was not on fleek. A great orator and writer, sure, but he wasn't going to win any beauty contests.

I love the fact that it was an ugly guy who God used to spread the news of God's Kingdom to Greece, a nation known for its obsession with beauty.

⟨⟨⟨⟨⟨⟩⟩⟩⟩⟩

Our American culture isn't much different than the Greeks when it comes to how highly we esteem beauty. We are similarly obsessed. It is what we use to sell beer and cars and potato chips and gadgets for the kitchen. Someone who has been thoroughly air-brushed is the one who is pitching our products, implying that if we were to possess the said product that we would either be admired and desired by such a perfect form of human perfection, or that this purchase will somehow bring us closer to becoming such an individual ourselves.

No worries if you aren't beautiful. Our consumer culture has that covered. There are cosmetic products to cover every flaw. And if you can't fool people in person, at least you can look your very best online. The internet is the perfect image-creating machine. Your picture can be photoshopped, airbrushed, and manipulated to make you a potential contestant in a beauty pageant.

Just don't let anyone see what you actually look like first thing in the morning.

It seems to me that this pressure is especially hard on women. It has been estimated that the average girl has seen over 77,500 ads by the time she reaches 12 years old. And it just gets worse the older you get. The corporate profiteers know just how to play upon our normal insecurity about our looks in order to get us to reach for our credit card.

At age 13, 53 percent of women are unhappy with their bodies, and by 17 that number spikes to 78 percent.

The standard is an impossible one. Barbie.

Problem is, nobody can actually reach that standard. Barbie's body shape cannot be achieved by a real human being.

Galia Slayen, a student at Hamilton College, once battled with body-image issues and an eating disorder. She realized that she had grown up thinking she should look like Barbie, so she decided to do an experiment. She created a life-sized model based on the toy doll. The results were disturbing. As she wrote on Huffington Post:

> If Barbie were an actual woman, she would be 5'9" tall, have a 39" bust, an 18" waist, 33" hips and a size 3 shoe…[She] would have a BMI of 16.24 and fit the weight criteria for anorexia.[1]

Here's the kicker: "She'd have to walk on all fours due to her proportions."

So, for all the little girls who say, "I want to look like Barbie when I grow up!"

You sure about that?

∞

It is heartbreaking to think of how many girls—and guys—have bought into this lie. A lie that sells products but doesn't bring happiness. A standard that is impossible and unrealistic. Let's dethrone the various Barbies of our culture. Let's remember that God chose an ugly dude to write much of the New Testament and to travel around the known world sharing good news about what really matters…

What's important is not how we look on the outside, but who we are on the inside.

Remember God's perspective. You are valuable. You are beautiful. Just as you are.

Stop listening to the lies.

My friend Cambria says that we aren't here to perfect our image so much as to reflect God's image. As someone made in the image of God you don't receive your value from the whims of advertisers. Your beauty comes from the fact that you have been created to reflect the very image of God.

God commanded people not to make graven images because He had already made images of Himself: you and me. Consequently, we see a guy walking a dog and say, "Oh, how cute! A puppy!" But God sees a guy walking a dog and responds, "Oh, how cute! A human!"

We are *Imago Dei*. The very image of God.

Image—God's image—is everything.

God sees you as a knockout, drop-dead beauty…just as you are.

He thinks you are "to die for."

And He did.

9

HOPE IS DOPE

You have probably figured out from all the quotes throughout this book that I love reading.

Reading has changed my life. While some people got their education by spending $60,000 for four years of college, I got most of mine through signing up for a library card. Nothing wrong with college, but you can spend a lot of money on education and still not be all that smart. But readers are leaders. And neuroscientists have discovered that reading is one of the best things for developing your brain.

If you become a reader it will open up your world, challenge your thinking, and equip you to be even more of an Optimisfit than you already are.

One book that I've found to be a particularly fascinating read is, you guessed it, the Bible.

Now, religion has done a lot of damage to the way people look at the Bible. The religious folks have turned it into a comprehensive rule book or into some sort of weird Ouija board that dispenses magic nuggets of wisdom. No wonder a lot of people have decided they just aren't interested.

No surprise there.

Religious people have a habit of twisting every good thing from God into something stale and boring and guilt-inducing. The Bible is no exception.

But honestly, I wonder if the religious people are actually *reading* the Bible. Because if they really were, they would be finding that it is not a list of regulations or a Magic 8 Ball. It is chock-full of and jam-packed with the promises of God. And since the living God is a God of hope, that means that His book is centered on hope. It is bubbling over with a frothy joy based upon that hope.

The Bible contains 1,189 chapters. Not every one of them is centered on the topic of hope, but that is the big overriding theme of the Good Book. The Bible contains 66 books, written by 40 different authors. Fourteen of them were written by the Apostle Paul. And in one of those is one of my very favorite verses. A verse that defines the whole Bible: "Everything that was written in the past was written for our instruction, so that through endurance and the encouragement of the Scriptures, we might have hope" (Romans 15:4).

There it is. *Bam.*

The central theme.

The Bible was given to us so that we might have hope.

Therefore, and this is *really important*, if you read the Bible and walk away with *less* hope rather than *more* hope, it's a giant exercise in missing the point.

Please read that last sentence again.

(((((O)))))

We suppose the Bible in our lap to be a book. But it is actually a library. There are many books inside. Most of the Bible is a story, but then there's a ton of poetry in there too. What's more, there's a memoir or two or three, legal code, genealogy, and loads of wisdom one-liners (an early form of Twitter?). There's even a play in the Bible. Of course, there are quite a few letters, a number of biographies of Jesus of Nazareth, a theological essay or two, not to mention a genre of literature we don't even have any more called apocalyptic. This library in your lap was penned over a period of a thousand years. It is the bestselling book of all time. It unflinchingly talks about the human condition: love, hate, war, injustice, when the church gets cozy with the empire, traumatic pain and healing, the meaning of existence, what to do with mold in your kitchen (don't forget that!), romance, the end of the world, doubt… you name it, it's all there.

Now, watch this…

About 43 percent of the Bible is narrative or story. And 33 percent is poetry. So, that means about 80 percent of the Bible is either a story or a poem, and less than 20 percent of Scripture is made up of straight-forward teaching. If you consider how much of the Bible is made up of direct commands, well, now we are down into the single digits.

That should change our whole approach to this book. It is not a legal document as much as a story and a poem. It's not intended to help us learn how to play by the rules. It is something much bigger than that. It is the beautiful story of how God sacrificed everything for you, His pearl of great price.

But since religious people like laws, many read the New Testament and try to turn it into a New Law. A new version of the old set of laws and commandments. They try to make Paul into Moses 2.0 and put all the focus on the dos and don'ts in his writings. And they miss the main message of "sonship," and freedom and hope.

We aren't set free so that we can be given a new set of shiny, fresh regulations for living.

We are set free to live. With God, and for God, and for one another.

(((())))

God is not a theology. He is a person.

And His book is not a systematic theology.

It is the unsystematic story of how crazy He is about you and me.

It is as wild and untamed as God Himself.

And with all the war and murder and sex, it isn't rated G. But it's a mighty good read.

10

CAMBRIA'S JOY

Some people just fit their name.

Cambria Joy is one of them. She simply sparkles. Her ear-splitting grin just lights up everything around her. I'm so grateful to be her friend. She's a key member of my Squad.

And she is kinda famous.

But that's no big deal with her. One day when she was still in her teens, Cambria sat down in front of her computer and created a simple little video blog about pretty ordinary stuff. It went viral. The thing is, she can talk about split ends or baby hairs or zucchini and it is all just plain fascinating.

She has become something of an internet star. Her blogs and videos get millions of hits, and she has her own following of fangirls, looking to her for advice on health, and happiness, and faith. Hanging on every word.

I'm a fan too. She and her husband, Bo, are two of my closest friends.

She has become my official little sister.

One of the things Cambria likes to talk about is body image. About how we are all held hostage to a bunch of unrealistic standards and goals about how we should look. It's a bondage that has trapped a lot of my generation. Advertising, movies, television, music—they all deliver a message that we aren't quite good enough to make the cut. That if we do this or buy that we'll be transformed into the perfect image that our culture is trying to sell us.

Somebody's getting rich by making us feel terrible about ourselves.

◯◯◯◯◯

Cambria reminds us that the goal of our lives shouldn't be about perfecting our body image, but about reflecting God's image.

Not by makeup, clothes, plastic surgery, or working to be as cool as possible.

Cambria is cool because she is just the person that she is.

She's got more charisma than DeNiro in *Godfather Part II*. And like him, she is larger than life.

Cambria is beautiful because she is lit up from the inside. God shines through her like almost no one else I know.

And Cambria is profound because she doesn't take herself too seriously. She loves a midnight trip to the local playground and enjoys playing on the slides meant for a five-year-old. She'll scream mock terror at the top of her lungs as she goes sliding down and collapse in a giggling heap at the bottom.

Five-year-olds don't give a lot of thought to fitting in with expectations or worry all that much about conforming. They just live at full-tilt, savoring every moment, and having the time of their lives.

That's what I like about five-year-olds.

That's what I like about Cambria.

11

THE WARDROBE EFFECT

If you are really paying attention you'll find that life is…magical.

When you step out the front door first thing in the morning ready to face the new day, you immediately are presented with the necessity of deciding what kind of world you are wandering into.

Is it the corporate world of the business-casual clothes, the weekly salary, and the thirst for the CEO's approval? Do you trudge forward with your umbrella tucked safely under your arm as you make your way to a job where you will drown yourself in the drudgery of yet another day? Along the way, are you guided by highway signs and billboards that seem identical no matter where you are? Do the golden arches of McDonald's offer your best promise of sustenance for your journey?

Or is it the secret country of Narnia that beckons you?

And does that umbrella double as a sword you can brandish in a swash-buckling manner as you do battle against boredom and complacency?

Just out of the line of sight, you know you exist in more than a world of binary code…

10010110011101010100001110

We are living in a wondrous world. A world where a child's laugh might give birth to a fairy.

Nature itself is as magical as the greatest fairy tales. It's a world where ducks wiggle their feet above the surface of the water as they perform a raucous headstand while diving for their next meal. Where kangaroos transport their young out of harm's way in the safety of belly pouches. Where macaque monkeys stuff their cheeks ridiculously full of food, making them look like some greedy young child from *Charlie and the Chocolate Factory*. Where parrots hold dialogues with their human pals.

It is a wondrous world. ✓

That's a truth that children know. ✓

And one that most adults have forgotten. ✓

⬤⬤⬤⬤⬤

In his book *Orthodoxy*, G.K. Chesterton reminds us of why this is so important. The reason we need fairy tales that tell us about a river that flows with gold, he says, is because we have forgotten how bizarre it is that rivers flow with water.

Our culture's picture of God is that of a Newtonian mathematician whose universe is a giant, logical, and sensible place where everything is done according to natural laws. It is a world marked by the monotony of a sun that rises and sets every day, just like clockwork.

Monotonous. That God is the Great Machinist who oversees a Great Machine.

Chesterton believed in a different kind of God, and so do I.

When I was a kid, my dad would put me on his shoulders as we played in the pool. We would submerge together, me crouching on his back as we sank slowly to the bottom. When his feet touched the floor of the pool he would push against it with all his might, launching us both upwards, and tossing me into the air, where I would splash down spread-eagled, causing the water to lap over the sides of the pool. As soon as I caught my breath I yelled, "Let's do it again!"

I could have done it all day.

I never got tired of it.

My desire for repetition was the exact opposite of monotony. Chesterton argued that God had that same childlike quality. He never got tired of sunrise and sunset, or of creating billions of daisies, all the same and yet each an original work of creative genius:

> Because children have abounding vitality, because they are in spirit fierce and free, therefore they want things repeated and unchanged. They always say, "Do it again"; and the grown-up person does it again until he is nearly dead. For grown-up people are not strong enough to exult in monotony. But perhaps God is strong enough to exult in monotony. It is possible that God says every morning, "Do it again" to the sun; and every evening, "Do it again" to the moon. It may not be automatic necessity that makes all daisies alike; it may be that God makes every daisy separately, but has never got tired of making them. It may be that He has the eternal appetite of infancy; for we have sinned and grown old, and our Father is younger than we.[2]

⟨⟨⟨⟩⟩⟩

An eight-year-old wants to read a story about how Harry opened a door and saw a dragon behind it.

A two-year-old is just amazed that Harry could open a door!

As we get older we are more interested in the materials the door is made of than in what might be behind it. We require ever more stimuli to remain interested. We grow indifferent to the wonder.

We become Muggles in a world of magic.

〇〇〇〇〇

We can pass through the wardrobe into the world of Narnia.

There is diversity to be found in a single drop of water. In the refracted glory of a rainbow streaking against the sky after the rains. In the dancing stars, the spinning planets, the spirals of the stretching galaxy.

We have brains capable of storing some 2,500,000 gigabytes of information—and turning that information into inventions, artistic creations, scientific theories, literary masterpieces, love notes, graduation speeches, rap songs, and a thousand other uses.

We come into the world with a supercomputer in our head.

And we quickly learn that there are quite a few things that are *beyond* that supercomputer.

The earth we live upon is a magical kingdom filled with enchanted forests and snowy peaks, upon which Gandalf and the Fellowship may be climbing even as our backs are turned. Maybe I'm a Romantic (I've been called worse things), but I sincerely believe there are gnomes in the garden and fairies in the flowers. I'm with the kids on this one.

And with George MacDonald, who also believed that flowers were fantastical things.

Jesus walked among the lilies and the mustard seeds, looking up at the doves and the sparrows, and He spoke of these in His teaching. He was paying attention. He saw the whole world as a temple of God, a place where we need to remove our shoes because we are treading on holy ground.

Some of today's scientists are in agreement when they remind us that it is better for our flesh-and-blood soles to make contact with the grass and the earth and the soil than to tread the world on the rubber soles of our shoes. It is, they say, vital to our health and well-being to make that kind of contact.

Our soles feed our souls.

(Insert groan.)

〇〇〇〇

Yes, this is Aslan's country all around us. It is harder to spot in the landscapes created by human beings—the highways and skyscrapers and shopping malls. But look close. Look up. Look around.

Look up and see the spine-tailed swift fly by at 105 miles per hour. How is that less magical than Harry Potter's broomstick?

I was recently speaking at an event in Southern California. I was trying to get in a nap before my talk was to begin. I stretched out on the hotel bed and closed my eyes. Just as I was starting to drift off, I heard a loud and persistent knocking outside. When I scrambled off the bed and answered it, there was nobody there. Before I could get settled I heard the knock again. Loud and impatient. I flung the door open. Still no one there. The third time this happened I stepped fully outside, only to discover a woodpecker just above the doorway.

What can you say about a creature who can bash its beak into wood in search of food without getting a headache, despite pecking up to 20 times per second?

Or what about the Arctic tern, a bird that migrates for 32,000 kilometers in its yearly journey from the Arctic to Antarctica and back? What kind of GPS is built into them, that they can return to the exact spot they left?

What kind of GPS for wonder is built within us?

We carry within us the wonder we seek around us.

⬭⬭⬭

While we live on this planet Earth we are also living on planet Narnia.

Aslan is still on the move.

The breath of the Great Lion still reanimates hearts that have been turned to stone.

And so, we venture from the safety of the front door each day to undertake an adventure in this strange and wonderful world of ours. And we find joy and meaning and awe in even the most mundane tasks we perform—because we see them as part of the epic story that is each of our own lives.

Remember Chesterton. He was a man who literally brandished his walking stick as if it were a sword. He was out for an adventure every single day.

How about you?

12

THE SCIENCE CHAPTER

Be careful.

You are about to step into fantastical territory.

What am I talking about? Stepping into Aslan's territory? A place where the sorting hat is singing? Where Hobbits are doing their merry jig? Or are we going to tumble down the rabbit hole?

Nope.

Welcome to Planet Earth. It is the most magical place of them all. It'll cast its spell on you.

Disclaimer: Read this chapter at your own risk. Its mixture of science and enchantment might just wreck you. If you read on, your ideas about your world might come apart at the seams.

But if you are brave enough to journey there, let's explore the magic of the Neverland we wake up in every morning.

There's a good reason why what we call *science* today, the ancients called *magic*. There isn't much difference between them when we drill down to the very deepest level. About 150 years ago, when quantum mechanics pulled the rug out from under Newtonian physics, we realized that we live in a much weirder universe than we had previously suspected. The old rules of materialism no longer applied. The world, we came to see, has more in common with Hogwarts than we thought.

Atoms are the keys that unlock these secrets because they make up, well, everything. And they play by their own rules.

Atoms are tinier than tiny. An atom compares in size to a golf ball as a golf ball compares to the whole planet. The nucleus of an atom is so dinky that if you blew up an atom to the size of a football stadium, its nucleus would be the size of a grain of rice. But here's the kicker. The grain of rice would weigh more than the stadium.

Does that blow your mind?

Well, I'm just getting started.

⬭⬭⬭⬭

Pick your jaw up off the floor and consider this:

Atoms are 99.9 percent empty space. If you removed all the empty space from all the atoms in the observable universe, the universe would fit inside a single sugar cube.

One lump or two?

What we see as solid is just an illusion. The rapidly swirling particles (made up mostly of empty space) are moving so fast that our eyes are tricked into registering the objects we see as solid. Everything we imagine to be stable is but a snow flurry of particles.

Tiny as they are, atoms are made up of even smaller building blocks, which we call subatomic particles. Scientists who study this stuff have counted more than 150 different kinds of subatomic particles. A veritable Particle Zoo.

The most famous of the subatomic particles is the electron. You were probably taught in school that electrons orbit the nucleus of the atom just as the planets in our galaxy orbit the sun. But what they do is actually quite a bit nuttier than that. They actually leap from point A to point B without traveling the distance in between. A quantum leap.

Which is really just a fancy term for teleportation. Or, maybe it's what Madeleine L'Engle called "a wrinkle in time."

Is your brain hurting yet?

An electron moves so fast that it can actually do 47,000 laps around a four-mile tunnel in one single second. And there are some electrons that can be spun 360 degrees and still not reveal their original face. You must spin them 360 degrees *twice* for them to return to that original position.

〇〇〇〇

The so-called laws of nature don't seem to apply to these little guys. Our "laws of nature" only apply to what we can observe…which is a very small part of the universe.

The universe itself disobeys the rules. Who knows if it isn't doing all kinds of funny things behind our backs when we aren't looking.

〇〇〇〇

There are subatomic particles that can exist in two places at the same time—that can literally pop into existence out of nowhere—and can be everywhere and nowhere at the same time.

Subatomic particles can communicate with each other, though we have no idea how. There is no signal. It's like telepathy or collective consciousness or something. If you turn a particle in Los Angeles it will turn a particle in New York in exactly the same way. They mirror each other even when separated. One theory is that they are traveling via quantum wormholes.

Just like a naughty child, subatomic particles change their behavior when they are being watched. They exist in ghost states and reveal the path they travel only when they are observed. This has led some to suggest that the universe itself can only exist when it is being watched. Couldn't this be used as an argument for the reality of God? An ever-present observer, *i.e.* God, is watching at all times. Everything is naked and exposed before His eyes. All things exist because He is looking.

Did you get all that?

Niels Bohr, the famous scientist, once said that if you are not outraged by hearing about quantum theory, then you aren't really understanding what is being said. It all sounds a little preposterous.

Werner Heisenberg discovered the uncertainty principle; namely, that you cannot predict both the position and the momentum of a quantum particle simultaneously. He once said something about all this that is probably my favorite quote about science:

"The first gulp of the rational sciences will make an atheist out of you, but God is waiting for you at the bottom of the glass."

Indeed.

A little bit of science asks questions that make an atheist out of some people, but if you delve a little deeper you'll find that there is more to the universe than meets the eye. We learn to ask different questions. Over the past few years I have done a lot of reading in advanced astrophysics and quantum mechanics. It has changed my perspective, and changed my life.

The sheer jaw-dropping strangeness and magical wonder of the universe convinces me that there is Someone behind it all. It's like the Wizard of Oz. There has to be Someone behind the curtain. Somewhere, out of sight, Someone is pulling the levers. Otherwise, it makes no sense.

Sir James Jeans, the famous physicist, wrote: "No astronomer can be an atheist." The screwy nature of outer space is more in line with believing in a God who breathes the stars into existence. Just like it says in the Psalms.

⬤⬤⬤⬤

It's a weird world.

Filled with charm and strangeness and mystery.

We live in a world where a flamingo can only eat when its head is upside down. Where an albatross can fly 25 miles an hour while sleeping. Where a three-toed sloth can turn its head nearly 360 degrees. Where an anglerfish has a fleshy lightbulb suspended from its forehead to help it capture food in the dark. Where there is a species of penguin only 16 inches tall. Where an emperor penguin slides along on his tuxedoed belly and dolphins surf waves. Where an In-N-Out Burger tastes like hope feels.

It's a weird and wild and wonderful world.

If you are tired of looking through the microscope, then look through a telescope. To the naked eye there are over 6,000 stars visible at night. But in actuality there are more than 100 billion stars in our galaxy. And billions of other galaxies beyond our own.

There is a celestial body out there called a neutron star that can weigh more than 200 billion tons (that's heavier than all the world's continents put together) and yet fit inside a teaspoon. There is a volcano on Mars. Some of Jupiter's moons are oblong rather than shaped like a perfect sphere.

Whether you are peering into a telescope or a microscope, what you'll see is a magical, wondrous, mind-blowing reality.

Sometimes I think that this world is more like the work of an amazingly imaginative artist than a by-the-rules engineer.

God's playfulness is on full display in the world He has made. It's a world tailor-made for the enjoyment of Optimisfits.

〇〇〇〇〇

Here is the Bible's scientific summary:

"In the beginning, God created the heavens and the earth" (Genesis 1:1).

Creation is an activity that belongs to God alone. The verb used in Hebrew is only used in the context of divine activity. Humans have never created something out of nothing. We can reassemble the particles in paint to bring about a work of art, or rearrange the vibrations to become a song, but actual creation is beyond us. J.R.R. Tolkien said that we are sub-creators, making something new out of elements that already exist. A songwriter friend told me that he doesn't create songs as much as he finds them. He said he is an archaeologist more than a songwriter. To write a song is to unearth an artifact.

The One who originally buried all these artifacts deep into the fabric of existence is the ultimate Composer, Painter, Sculptor, and Writer. All we do is discover what He put there for us to find.

Light is everywhere in the universe. Even in black holes, dark matter, and dark energy. Light is in the places that appear darkest.

The Apostle John tells us that "God is light." He is everywhere. Even in the darkness of the valley of the shadow of death. I know an eight-year-old who was told by a skeptical adult, "I'll give you an orange if you can tell me where God is." The child thought just a moment and replied: "I'll give you ten oranges if you can tell me where God is not."

Just because you can't see light doesn't mean it's not there.

Like light, God is everywhere. Omnipresent even in the darkest places and spaces. Just because you can't see something doesn't mean it's not there.

Consider electricity. It is invisible, but you can see its effects if you are fool enough to stick a fork in an electrical socket. Sparks are not electricity, only its effects. You can't see the wind, but you can see its effects. A dust devil is not the wind, but rather an effect of the wind. And when you toss a basketball in the air and it comes careening back down to the court you are not actually seeing gravity, only its effect.

The Bible puts it this way: We walk by faith, not by sight.

I can't see God, but every day I can see His effects.

Creation testifies of a Creator. When I see the *Mona Lisa*, I don't think it is just an accidental by-product of fortuitous events. I see da Vinci. When I see the miraculous world that surrounds us, I see God's fingerprints all over it.

13

THE DRAGONS BEHIND THE DOOR

We live in a world of wonders, but it is so very easy to become jaded.

As we get older we become accustomed to the miracles that surround us. We lose the magic. We lose the wonder.

As we get older we stand in front of the door but we don't bother to open it because we think we already know what is behind it.

Many blame the popular version of scientific thinking like you see on TV documentaries for this diminution of a sense of wonder. And yes, there is a certain kind of scientific thinker who is not really as interested in *explaining* as in *explaining away*.

But the pursuit of real science increases the sense of wonder. We realize that we are surrounded by mysteries.

Religion is often like that popular version of science. When it pretends that the awesome mystery of God can be reduced to a handful of theological propositions or a list of moral precepts or a defense of Western culture…then religion is every bit as reductionist as the worst kind of science.

But real spirituality, real faith, real theology…these embrace the mystery and live in the joy of constant discovery of the deeper places God wants to take us.

⦅⦆

It drives me cuckoo when religion puts itself forward as being against science and against logic and against open-minded thinking. The questions aren't very meaningful when you already think you have all the answers.

It leads to all kinds of evils. It forbids people like Galileo and Copernicus from showing us the splendor of the solar system. It threatens any fresh thinking that goes against the official *interpretation* of the Bible. These greatest scientists of the past weren't questioning the Bible, just the current *interpretation* of their time, which we now know was *wrong*.

When religious thinking refuses to keep learning, it gets in the way of progress.

It turns away people who value thinking deeply about things. Successful people, it has been said, have small TVs and large libraries, and failures have small libraries and big TVs. That is probably an overstatement…and I do like my wide-screen television. But there is a lot of truth hidden in that overgeneralization.

Read more. Keep your mind open. Pay attention.

But don't just read the stuff you know will support what you already believe.

When it comes to keeping the mind awake and open, Optimisfits don't believe in playing it safe.

Let your mind wander among the wonders.

Be like that child who is fascinated about how things work and who expects a surprise behind every closed door.

You can't do that if you have a closed mind.

14

MY HEROES

Some of the most important members of my Squad are no longer alive.

And no, they aren't undead zombies.

They no longer happen to be walking around on this planet, but their influence continues to be felt. They are Optimsfits all, even if the term didn't exist in their day. They have taught me how to think and how to live and how to ask better questions.

So, cue the music. Here are a few of the members of my Optimisfit Hall of Fame:

He was the jolly journalist who wrote an unbelievable number of books during his lifetime. He made the writing look effortless because of his genius. He penned books defending the reasonableness of the faith, biographies of famous saints and literary figures, poetry, wild and fantastical fiction, and wry mystery novels. He was quick with an argument and even quicker with a witty insight. He was bigger than life, not only in reputation, but also in stature. Well-rounded in every sense of the word. A fat, jolly British Santa Claus of metaphysics.

He was G.K. Chesterton.

Like any good Optimisfit, he knew that this world was also Elfland—a world of mystery and magic, and he was like Gandalf striding its environs. And Chesterton was serious enough to know that you can't take everything too seriously…and he didn't.

Chesterton loved to defend the truth against all comers, and one of his famous antagonists was the skinny and skeptical playwright, George Bernard Shaw. The two of them would debate publicly about faith and other important issues, much to the delight of the audiences who came to see them cross their verbal swords. Once, Chesterton remarked on Shaw's emaciated form by saying, "I see there has been a famine in the land." Shaw looked Chesterton up and down and said, "And I see the cause of it." "If I were as fat as you," added Shaw, "I would hang myself." To which Chesterton countered, "If I were to hang myself, I would use you as the rope."

Chesterton was an intellectual genius, but that didn't make him snooty or arrogant. It made him childlike. He knew the wisdom to be found in fun, and the folly in taking yourself too seriously. "Angels can fly," he once wrote, "because they take themselves lightly."

He never minded when his opinions made him controversial. He quipped, "I believe in getting into hot water; it keeps you clean."

◎◎◎◎

When I am not writing books like the one you are reading, I am working on my still-unfinished epic fantasy novel. In that way I am a little like another of my misfit heroes—a man who wrote both inspiring literary sermons and imaginative fairy tales. He got kicked out of his job as a pastor because some members of the board of elders thought he put too much emphasis on God's love. He believed that God was more generous and grace-filled than some people's "orthodox" theology could accommodate.

He was George MacDonald.

When the leaders of organized religion took away his pulpit, he used the pages of books as his way of sharing his theological musings about God's profligate love. He wrote books for adults, but his greatest books are the ones he wrote for children—or maybe we should say that they are fairy tales for the child in each of us.

I'm not alone in my love for George MacDonald. He was C.S. Lewis' favorite writer, and Lewis once claimed that he had never written a book that didn't quote from MacDonald. In fact, it was a book by MacDonald that "baptized the imagination" of the man who would come to write the Narnia stories; the first step toward the light for C.S. Lewis. Lewis repaid the debt by making MacDonald the wise spiritual guide through the afterlife in *The Great Divorce*. And he always referred to MacDonald as "my master."

MacDonald once said, "Man finds it hard to get what he wants because he does not want the best; God finds it hard to give because He would give the best, and man will not take it." His mission was to help people understand that what God offered was magnificent, and that we must receive it with a heart of childlike wonder. He once quipped that he couldn't really believe in someone's Christianity if children could never be found playing around their front door.

God's revelation could be found, he believed, not just in the ancient texts of Scripture, but in the magic of the stars, the sunset, and the daffodil. When a person sees things as they really are, they will see the holiness at the heart of the ordinary. Whereas false visions make commonplace things seem more ordinary, true visions reveal the extraordinariness of commonplace things.

MacDonald wrote fantasy stories because he believed that *this* world is truly fairyland. And when I read his books I sense the truth of that belief. I can feel the Presence of something bigger rustling through every page. Or should I say, Some*one* bigger?

(OOOO)

One of my more down-to-earth Optimisfit heroes was the greatest evangelist of our time; a man who shared the Good News with millions of people. His message was simple, his delivery was passionate, and his results were astonishing. So many people owe their introduction to Jesus to this man.

He was Billy Graham.

He made a point of never criticizing those who believed differently than he did. Early in his career as a preacher he was known as "machine-gun Billy" because he talked so fast, but he only turned that machine gun on people's hearts, with a message of good news about God's love.

He refused to allow his crusades to be segregated, tearing down the barriers separating blacks and whites at a time when most Christians hadn't awakened to the evils of racism. He refused to pay attention to the squabbles between the different denominations, and even put Catholic priests on the podium with him. He was heeding the prayer of Jesus, that all His followers would be one. Some criticized him harshly, but he was not a man of convenience; he was a man of conviction.

I guess I have modeled my own speaking style after him. I love how he would roll up his sleeves and his eyes would start to burn with a piercing blue gaze of intensity. He used his whole body to gesture and emphasize his points. Passion like that always offends milquetoast mediocrity. I hope I can do the same. Billy always gave his all for the gospel. He had an amazing work ethic and a total focus on his mission. Long before he stood in front of crusade-sized crowds he would preach to the local alligators for practice! (True story.)

Faith can move mountains, but don't be surprised when God hands you a shovel.

⬭⬭⬭⬭

My final Optimisfit hero in the Hall of Fame was a blond-haired Macedonian who believed that he was a son of a god, and he outraced the winged chariot of time by conquering most of the known world by the age of 32. He traveled with his personal copy of Homer's *Iliad* in his pack and would often fall asleep reading about the exploits of Achilles, who was his own model for surpassing even the exploits of the gods. He saw himself, in fact, as a reincarnation of Achilles, just as Patton believed he was a Viking in a previous life. He was fearless and heroic and dreamed outsized dreams.

He was Alexander the Great.

He roared with authority. He was savage, not average. He was unrelenting, driving his army to the brink of exhaustion in pursuit of the prize. He once said, "I am not afraid of an army of lions which are led by a sheep; I am afraid of an army of sheep which are led by a lion." He took the fight to his enemies.

In that way, Alexander models the One whom Scripture dubs the "Captain of Salvation." Jesus told His disciples that the Gates of Hell would not prevail against those who followed Him. But consider this. Gates don't attack. When you grab a weapon for battle, you don't use a gate. You don't hoist a gate and yell threateningly, "Here I come!" No, you take a sword or an axe or a bow and arrow. A gate is not a weapon. So what Jesus was saying is that we are to go on the *offense*. We are to be on the attack against the powers of darkness.

Optimisfits don't just stand by and watch the enemy do his work. We don't cower. We don't try to negotiate terms with darkness.

We are never hopeless. We are always fearless. We pour water on the fire of our fears. We pour gasoline on the passions of our dreams.

The more people told Alexander that something was impossible, the more attracted he was to the challenge. He had an absurdly buoyant hope.

Yes, Alexander was probably clinically insane. But those who are crazy enough to think they can change the world are the ones who actually do. Realistic people don't change the world. Maybe we all could do with being a little less sane. What we need is not more bored realism, but more wild idealism.

It's better to attempt great things for God and fail than to attempt small, safe things, and succeed.

Alexander became a legend. Which sounds like a pretty good goal. We Optimisfits want to live in legendary mode. We can take the battle to the enemy and claim the crowns of victory in the Kingdom of God.

We were made for thrones, not graves.

◌◌◌◌◌

None of my heroes chose the safe route. None of them were normal. None of them settled for small successes. So, if life is a battle, let's take our place alongside our Heavenly King. We are childlike, we are faithful, we are brave.

And we are just a little foolhardy…in the best possible way.

DO NOT READ THIS CHAPTER

DO NOT READ THE NEXT SENTENCE!!!

I'm warning you!!!

You little rebel. I like you. Welcome to Dauntless.

#nourishyourinnerrebel #zerofear #factiondauntless

MY DAD IS
CHUCK NORRIS

My dad is Chuck Norris.

Well, not literally. But he looks a lot like him and he has the same kind of muscular physique. He likes to wear those tank tops that show off his "guns." ("Sun's out, guns out.") During my childhood, *Walker, Texas Ranger* was one of the most popular programs on TV, and Dad was a dead ringer for the mighty Chuck Norris, who starred in that show. Norris could always stride with confidence into even the most uncertain of situations and set things right with his imposing stature and fearless demeanor.

Sadly, I am nothing like my dad.

As a kid I got beat up a lot by a bully who lived on the same block.

Her name was *Samantha*, and she loved putting me in my place.

As I grew older, I continued to attract bullies. After all, I was skinny, had a voice that caused me to be mistaken for a girl at the Taco Bell drive-thru, and I couldn't bench press much more than the bar itself.

Despite all that, I never lost a fight.

I never lost a fight because I always ran away.

I fled for my life.

Fortunately, my school was only a block from my home. So, when a bully would threaten me I'd run to my dad for protection. In the presence of my dad, I became fearless. Even a bit cocky.

"You got a problem with me? Take it up with him," I'd say. "You aren't that intimidating. Go ahead, take a long walk off a short pier," I'd threaten, or something along those lines.

One look at my dad and the bullies would retreat.

◌◌◌◌◌

When David faced off against the giant Goliath he taunted him as "an uncircumcised Philistine," which was an example of ancient trash talk. Similarly, I could fearlessly taunt the bullies when my dad was nearby. Though I was a hopeless fighter myself, I had all the confidence in the world when my father had my back.

Nothing much has changed.

Based on my own courage I am still not going to get very far. But my Heavenly Father is one seriously focused fighter.

In Romans 8:37, Paul said that through the love of the Father we are "more than conquerors." In the original Greek language, the phrase literally means that we are "super-overcomers." All because we can lean on the One who is braver than Batman, stronger than Superman, more indomitable than Ironman, more audacious than Antman. His name is the "Son of Man" and He is the warrior (Exodus 15:3) and He's fighting battles on our behalf and answering prayers at our behest. I cannot lose. I may fail from time to time, but ultimately, I will never lose. For His love never fails.

Yeah, One greater than Chuck Norris is beside me.

And I am a superhero.

My superpowers are trust and dependence.

Marvel and D.C. should be looking me up any day.

17

PRAYERS AT MIDNIGHT

I like to walk through the city at night, rambling along under the lights and the stars with no particular destination in mind. This is when I do some of my best praying.

I mosey along through the quiet streets and talk to God about the things that are on my heart.

My prayers aren't necessarily the noble ones about orphans in Gambia. Often, they are more like sharing gossip with a good friend. I talk to Him about the people I love as well as the people who really bug me. I tell Him about my girl problems, insecurities, nagging questions, and my deepest dreams.

He tells me that my dreams can only fully come into focus once I have put aside my fear.

Message received.

Now, some of you will take me for a nut job if I tell you that God talks back to me. But He does.

In my defense, consider what Mother Teresa said in an interview with Dan Rather. He asked her: "When you talk to God, what do you say?"

"I don't say anything," she answered. "I listen."

"When God talks to you, what does He say?"

"He doesn't say anything," she replied. "He listens."

Rather looked confused, so she said, "And if that doesn't make sense to you, I can't explain it."

Boom.

A lot of the best things really can't be explained.

Deep calls unto deep.

∞

Research shows that few things are as good for your brain as the regular practice of prayer. Not only does it help you feel closer to God, but it also fires the frontal lobe of the brain and engages our highest intellectual capabilities.

Yep. Prayer actually makes you smarter.

Who knew?

Well, God did.

∞

Sometimes I don't bother actually talking with Him about anything specific. We just walk the streets together underneath the glowing street lamps and the blinking traffic lights and all the stars twinkling in the velvet night sky.

When you are really in love, sometimes there are just no words.

And sometimes that is the best kind of praying.

18

NARNIAN ROYALTY

Here's a bit of useful trivia: Do you know which verse resides in the exact middle of the Bible?

Here it is: "It is better to trust in the Lord than to put confidence in princes" (Psalm 118:9 kjv).

I think that helps explain the attitude of Optimisfits toward politics. We know that governments will always ultimately fail us. After all, they are composed of fallible human beings. And politicians are usually more about image than substance. That "image" is about as real as the one you craft for yourself on social media.

Can I get another like? 👍

If you are waiting for the donkeys and elephants to solve all the world's problems and usher in a new time of peace and prosperity, you are going to have a very long wait.

Some people are all about the right wing, and others are all about the left wing, but I think that God is all about the whole bird! What's more, He *is* the bird. He has lifted us up on eagle's wings according to Exodus 19:4.

God's Kingdom is not *from* this world, but it is *for* this world, just as we are *in* the world, but not *of* the world. It is a Kingdom that comes down from heaven to make a difference on the earth below. His goal is not just to get us into heaven, but to get heaven into us.

◎◎◎◎

The Bible uses political terms to describe God's reign among us. When Jesus calls Himself the Son of God, He is using a term that was often ascribed to Caesar Augustus. This term, *Divi Filius*, was even inscribed on some Roman coins right next to his picture.

In fact, it was widely believed among Romans that Emperor Caesar ascended to heaven to sit at the right hand of the gods. So, you can see why it was so dangerous for Luke to write that Jesus had ascended to the right hand of God. Caesar Domitian had a choir who often followed him around chanting, "You are worthy our Lord and God, to receive glory and honor and power." Which is exactly what John records is spoken around the throne of God in the book of Revelation. These New Testament writers were rebels. They were the resistance movement. It is no wonder that the Empire tried to kill them off.

So, when people said that Jesus was the Son of God, they were proclaiming that He was the King rather than Caesar. Dangerous, dangerous. Today, when we talk about the "gospel" we are actually hijacking a political propaganda term used by the Romans to proclaim the reign of the emperor. It proclaimed that they had brought about peace through their military triumphs. Their common phrase for this accomplishment was "Peace Through Victory." The Roman peace (*Pax Romana*) was sustained through the shedding of the blood of every challenger.

Jesus proclaimed a different kind of Kingdom.

His message was the opposite of the Roman motto. His motto was "Victory Through Peace."

He didn't conquer the earth by bathing the world in the blood of His enemies; He overcame the world by bathing His enemies with His own blood.

◯◯◯◯

We have a special place in that Kingdom.

We're not seated in the cheap seats or the nosebleed section. We are seated in the heavenly places!

We are the Kings and Queens of Narnia. Paul calls us "God's elect" and John refers to us as "kings." We are also spoken of as "ambassadors," the emissaries and representatives of the Great High King, the God of Hope. And one day, the Bible tells us, we will be given thrones. We are destined to rule and reign with Him. Now that is what I call upward mobility.

And this perspective changes the way we should think about the political struggles of our own day. It doesn't mean that we ignore the important issues or refuse to get involved when we need to, but it provides a perspective that reminds us that politics is not the ultimate answer to every problem.

We understand that there is a higher authority than monarchy, oligarchy, autocracy, or even democracy. We are participating in a theocracy, where God rules.

Our job is to find whatever doesn't represent heaven on earth, and, well, vanquish it!

So, if there are problems in life that you cannot solve, remember that it is kind of like your old math textbooks in school—the answers are in the back of the book. The book of Revelation reminds us that as the future unfolds, we can trust in the One who holds that future in His hands. God is on the throne, and He is the King of kings. In 17 of the 22 chapters of Revelation we get a glimpse of God on the throne; there are roughly 45 occasions where John gives us a glimpse of God perched in the place of ultimate power.

The elders around that throne fall to their knees and proclaim His judgments to be "righteous." We join them. Like the surfing turtle in *Finding Nemo*, we ride the currents and hoot, "Righteous!"

And when we look back at our lives someday, we'll see how God has been at work. We'll say, "Righteous! It all makes sense now! Everything You did in my life was perfect. Righteous and true are Your judgments, O King!"

God isn't messing around when it comes to His rule. As my friend Levi likes to say, "There's no game when it comes to *His* throne."

19

WALT DISNEY HAS NO GOOD IDEAS

Early in his struggling career as a newspaper cartoonist, Walt Disney was fired because the editor-in-chief said, "Disney lacks imagination and has no good ideas."

Once he decided to start making animated films, most of his early ones failed to find much of an audience. He could barely survive on the pittance he earned with these cartoons. Long after most people would have just given up, he finally broke through with a little cartoon called *Steamboat Willie* which starred a mouse name Mickey. This changed everything.

But Disney wouldn't settle for making successful cartoons. He wanted to stretch himself to do something new and unique. He decided to create a place where families could come and share in imaginative adventures together. It would be a magical theme park called *Disneyland*. Few thought it a viable idea. Most thought he was just an unrealistic dreamer.

When he tried to get funding for this idea, he was turned down by over a hundred banks.

Eventually he was able to build the park, which was an unmitigated disaster on its opening day. But he persevered with his vision. Today, "The Happiest Place on Earth" is one of the most popular vacation destinations in the world.

Disney had plenty of opportunities to give up. But he didn't.

He had no fear of failure.

⬭⬭⬭

Colonel Sanders, the country gentleman with a white suit that matched his white hair, founded Kentucky Fried Chicken, but only after being turned down by over a thousand restaurants to which he tried to sell his secret recipe of "11 herbs and spices."

When it came to facing failure, he wasn't a chicken.

⬭⬭⬭

Charlie Chaplin's initial screen tests were not encouraging. The film company concluded that his act "was too obscure for people to understand." It didn't happen overnight, but eventually he became America's first bona fide movie star.

Thomas Edison's schoolteachers thought him too stupid to learn anything.

Beethoven's music teachers told him he was hopeless when it came to composition.

Dr. Seuss had the manuscript for his first book rejected by 27 publishers.

Harrison Ford was told by a movie executive that he didn't have what it takes to make it in the movie business.

Vincent Van Gogh was a prolific painter, but he sold a grand total of one painting in his entire life.

Abraham Lincoln had an almost impossible time getting into law school, failed twice at business ventures, lost eight elections, and had a nervous breakdown. All before he became our sixteenth president.

(((((())))))

Winston Churchill lost nearly every election he participated in and was considered a failure and a has-been before he finally and unexpectedly became the Prime Minister of Britain in his sixties.

He had failed sixth grade.

He famously defined success as having the ability to go from one failure to the next without losing enthusiasm. That was the story of his life. Failure was his jam.

Someone once asked him about the qualifications for being a politician. His answer:

> A politician needs the ability to foretell what is going to happen tomorrow, next week, next month, and next year. And to have the ability afterwards to explain why it didn't happen.[3]

Failing is an inescapable part of living life in legendary mode.

(((((())))))

In her bestselling book, *The 5 Second Rule*, Mel Robbins hit it on the head:

> Do you know the game Angry Birds? Rovio, the brand that created the game launched fifty-one unsuccessful games before they

developed Angry Birds. How about the *Avengers* star Mark Ruffalo? Do you know how many auditions he did before he landed his first role? Almost 600! Even Babe Ruth struck out 1,330 times. My favorite vacuum cleaner is Dyson…James Dyson created 5,127 prototypes. What? And this last one will blow your mind. Picasso created nearly 100 masterpieces in his lifetime. But what most people don't know is that he created a total of more than 50,000 works of art. 50,000. That's two pieces of art a day.[4]

This ratio of masterpieces to artistic failures doesn't sound very promising. But Picasso failed his way into greatness.

(((())))

When we look at the heroes of the Bible we see the same pattern: success only comes after major failure.

Moses originally had no confidence in himself as a leader and speaker. And he had serious issues with his temper. But he led his people out of Egyptian slavery.

Elijah could become almost suicidal when depression descended upon him, but he was the greatest of the prophets.

Paul had made a career out of killing Christians before he became the most prolific writer of the New Testament.

Peter had a talent for saying the wrong thing at the wrong time. Then he denied Jesus at the most critical moment. But he became the Rock upon which Jesus built His church.

David's lustful desires for the wife of one of his soldiers led him to orchestrate that man's death, yet he came to be called "a man after God's own heart."

Rahab practiced the oldest profession, but she still makes the Hebrews 11 "Hall of Faith."

These were no white knights or shiny superheroes. They were failures all.

But they failed forward.

Their failures were not the end of their stories.

◯◯◯◯

These stories of heroic failure give me hope that it is worth it to keep picking myself up after I mess up, and keep taking new risks so that I am always moving forward. Patton said, "It ain't about how high you climb, it's about how high you bounce when you hit the bottom."

If you are afraid of failure you'll never realize your dreams.

Failing makes your story interesting. I'm just bored when I hear a guy talk about how every shot he put up went in. *Yawwwwn.*

The best stories are about perseverance in the face of challenge, about how someone rises like a phoenix from the ashes of defeat, about how people respond to rock bottom.

I always love a comeback.

I'm counting on experiencing them.

In the meantime, God loves you right where you are. He loves you just as much when you're at your lowest moment as He is at your peak performance.

Look no further than Jesus. When He was baptized in the Jordan River, near the Dead Sea, which was the lowest elevation on planet Earth, God proclaimed Him to be His Beloved Son. Then, when He was transfigured on the top of Mount Hermon (the highest mountain in all of Israel), God once again repeated that statement—that He was the Beloved Son.

When we are at the peak, we are beloved, just like Jesus.

When we are in the lowest valley, we are beloved, just like Jesus.

When Elijah was strong in faith the Bible says that the ravens fed him and a widow sustained him. But later, when he was at his lowest point, wracked with doubts and feeling like a failure, it says that *angels* waited upon him and *God Himself* fed him.

Sometimes God works through our doubts more than through our faith. When we reach the end of ourselves we find a new beginning with God. What starts out as an air ball that completely misses the hoop becomes something that God can use as an alley-oop to throw down on our enemy.

◯◯◯◯

It is said that the average person makes 35,000 choices every day.

I make a lot of dumb ones.

But God adores me and forgives me, which means that even my worst failures—and yours—can't separate us from His love. He loves you so, so, so, so much. And He gleefully forgives you. Therefore, none of your failures can keep you from your destiny.

Irving Stone spent his life studying great men and women, and turning the results of his research into novelized biographies. Two of the most popular featured Michelangelo and Van Gogh. When he was asked if he'd found any sort of thread that runs through the lives of the great people he'd written about, he replied:

> I write about people who sometime in their life…have a vision or dream of something that should be accomplished…and they go to work. They are beaten over the head, knocked down, vilified and for years they get nowhere. But every time they are knocked down they stand up. You cannot destroy these people. And at the end of their lives they have accomplished some modest part of what they set out to do.[5]

I vibe with that.

Hebrews 11 gives us the "Hall of Faith."

Maybe we need an Optimisfit's "Hall of Faith and Failure." It would include a lot of the people we've talked about in this chapter. People who kept failing until they found their way to their dreams.

It would include me.

And you.

20

10,000 HOURS

A few years ago, a report was released which revealed that the average young person spends a lot of time with entertainment devices. Shocking information, huh? Between video games, television, and surfing the internet, the average came to more than seven-and-a-half hours per day. That's 53 hours per week. Older people clocked only a slightly smaller number of hours.

Let's be honest about what that means. We are killing an awful lot of time consuming entertainment, battling virtual adversaries, or stewing about the latest news being delivered on the 24-hour cable networks.

Neurologists tell us that bad news sticks to the brain like Velcro, whereas good news slips out of our noggins like water through a sieve. Nine people say something nice on your Instagram feed, and one person says something mean. What do you spend your time thinking about? The bad news sticks, which is why it is not a good idea to accumulate a whole lot of bad news.

Since bad news sells, the networks run the negative stories over and over. Their feed repeats every 30 minutes. The threats. The conspiracies. The accusations. The fearmongering. No wonder we get depressed by watching too much of it.

But we are hooked.

Another study found that most people check their cell phone every six minutes…or 150 times per day, searching for the rush of dopamine that social media produces. I have a lot of people who *like* me, we tell ourselves. Just check my Facebook feed.

We are all in grave danger of iDolatry.

And there are billions of websites out there in the ether, offering us endless information and cat videos. People used to read books by knowledgeable specialists, looking for a depth of understanding that comes from studying the printed page. Now we can skim a series of posts by random bloggers and think we understand. It just seems like a more fun way to learn, right? It takes less effort, even though we must burn a whole lot of time trying to sort the dependable truths from the fraudulent half-truths.

We spend over 50 hours a week watching TV, playing games, surfing the net, or checking our social media. This doesn't leave a lot of time for actual *living*.

⦅⦆

Optimisfits don't want to waste our time on things that don't really matter.

⦅⦆

You might be tired of hearing about how much I dislike rules, so here is a good rule, one that I totally believe every Optimisfit will find is worth following…

It is the 10,000-hour rule.

The concept comes from Malcolm Gladwell's book *Outliers*. He argues that the only way to find success at anything is to invest time in it. A lot of time. At least 10,000 hours.

Gladwell makes the case that whether it be Steve Jobs or Bill Gates, Wolfgang Mozart or Bobby Fischer, Arnold Palmer or Michael Jordan—you only get really good at something by focusing on your goals and working hard to achieve them. He found that the real successes were the people who were willing to invest 10,000 hours on their "thing," whatever that thing might be.

For some it is the latest version of Halo. By the age of 21, the average American has put over 10,000 hours of practice in computer gaming.

Consider the Beatles. If you have heard their earliest recordings, you'll know that they weren't very good when they first started making music. In fact, they were pretty much terrible. But they took a gig at a run-down club in Hamburg, Germany, where they played eight hours a day for seven days a week. They did this for months on end. (It probably felt like "Eight Days a Week"!) They played more shows before the famous British invasion than most bands do in their entire career. They put in countless hours perfecting their performances and enhancing their musicianship and when they finally started recording, it seemed like a miracle. Their records became instant chart toppers. Their live show took Britain and America by storm.

It takes thousands of hours of practice to become an overnight success.

Chris Martin, the lead singer and lyricist for the band Coldplay, says that the secret to writing a great song is just putting in the hours. He often stays up all night, writing and rewriting, working and reworking the music and the words until sometimes he literally falls asleep with his head on the piano keys.

Professional golfers will tell you that it is only hours of repeated practice that makes their shots look so effortless. Basketball greats will tell you about how much time they spend practicing at the free throw line so they can make it "nothing but net" in crunch time.

All too often we spend a lot of time waiting for our opportunity to turn up. Instead, we should turn up our sleeves and get to work.

Too many people have a million-dollar dream and a minimum-wage work ethic.

Charles Spurgeon said that if we focus on our ability, then God will take care of the opportunity.

The way we triumph is to add a little *umph* to our try.

One of my heroes is John Wesley, who preached 42,000 sermons during the course of his life. (Do the math; that's three sermons a day on average!) He traveled 60 to 70 miles a day on horseback to share the message of God's love with people in far-flung locations. When he was 83 years old he was able to write in his diary: "I am a wonder to myself. I am never tired either with preaching, writing, or traveling."

Little surprise that he changed the world.

I've tried to follow that kind of example. While I was still in my twenties I had written three books, had a weekly television show with a global outreach, and a radio program on 400 stations. And I've travelled all over the world, speaking to groups large and small.

Since I am still pretty young, people are surprised at how comfortable I am in front of a crowd or a camera. Well, it isn't by accident. Young as I am, I have been doing this for a long time. I started early, I worked hard, and I kept at it.

I recently calculated that I have invested more than 11,000 hours in honing my craft as a writer and speaker. I still work about 13 hours a day on writing, reading, and speaking. I consume books as fast as I can, especially those related to what I love to talk about.

If that all sounds like a terrible grind, well, it isn't. It is amazing how much fun it is to do the things you really care about.

And when I'm done working, I play hard.

I play *hard*.

My friend Peter told me that in order for a Chinese bamboo tree to grow, you must water it every day for five years. In those five years you'll see no growth. Not even a bud. But if you miss even one day of watering, that bamboo tree is likely to die. After five years of consistently watering it every single day, though, it will then grow 80 feet in 42 days.

My secret to success isn't that I'm smart. In fact, I'm dumb by nature. I had a 2.0 GPA in school. No one picked me for "most likely to succeed." But I think I have managed to rewire my brain by working hard. I've built intellectual muscle and spiritual muscle by focusing on my growth in those areas.

It all begins with your thoughts.

Here's a quote that I love. No one really knows where it originated, but it offers a great blueprint for life: "When you sow a thought, you reap an action; when you sow an action you reap a habit; when you sow a habit you reap a character; and when you sow a character you reap a destiny."

The thoughts you think become the words you say, which become the actions you undertake, which create the habits you form, which transform your lifestyle. But it all begins with the thoughts we think.

Follow your heart, but make sure your brain always comes along for the ride.

21

RUNNING FREE

It should have been my moment of glory.

It was the first game of the season for my eighth-grade basketball team, the South Medford Generals. I was excited to be able to demonstrate my prowess with the ball, as I had worked hard all summer to bring my game to the next level.

On the first play of the game, the ball was tipped into my hands. I lowered my head and dribbled past the defender, a bit surprised at how easily I was able to get past him. It seemed like he wasn't even bothering to guard me. I drove to the hoop and put the ball up. I kissed it off the glass. It fell through the net.

Two points.

For the other team.

I'd put the ball in the wrong basket. So, I started my breakout season with negative two points.

So much for my moment of glory.

By the end of the season it didn't matter. My team won the Rogue

Valley championship anyway. In the finals we had a showdown against our crosstown rivals and shut them down decisively. It wasn't even close. We cooked 'em. The officials placed the gold medals around our necks and we posed for the obligatory photos, filled with the pride of achievement.

But let me tell you, I didn't have much to do with our success. Sometimes, like the debacle of my first game, I think I actually made it harder for us to win. The reason we made it to the finals and became champs was mainly because we had this kid on our team named Kyle Singler.

Kyle was a talent to behold.

He went on to get a full-ride scholarship to Duke University, where he won a championship under Coach K. He was named the Final Four "player of the game." He was drafted by the Detroit Pistons and was elected to the second team All-NBA rookie squad. Today, he's raking in nearly five million dollars every year playing for the Oklahoma City Thunder as a professional NBA basketball player.

He was on my team.

A couple of years ago I ran into my old basketball coach and said, "Wasn't it great when we had Kyle on our team?"

"Oh yeah," he replied. "Our whole game strategy was just give the ball to Kyle."

⟨⟨⟨⟩⟩⟩

Sometimes winning is all about who is on your Squad.

Though I sometimes still score for the wrong team, the Captain of Salvation is on my team. I am often awful, but my God is never anything other than awesome. He is the star player who assures how the final score is going to look.

When the final buzzer goes off there is no question that we will have won.

Even if, at this very moment, we are trailing, we don't have to worry. We will pull this off.

That, my friends, is the basis of hope.

No matter how much I mess things up, no matter how bad the situation might be, no matter how much it feels like I am trapped in a corner and things don't look good—my hope is in a God who says that the battle belongs to Him. He has never lost yet.

The game is rigged. In our favor.

(((())))

Some cynics will tell you that hope is illogical.

But I believe hope is the most sensible thing in the world. My hope is not an empty hope. It isn't wishful thinking. It isn't about positive confession. It isn't trying to convince myself that something is true that I have my doubts about.

My hope is certain.

It is based on facts. Hope is not hype. God has proven Himself again and again in my life and in the lives of others. He will fight on my behalf, He will champion my cause, He will see me through. Because He has overcome the world.

Period.

Hope isn't an airy-fairy, happy-clappy, wishy-washy pie-in-the-sky matter. In the Old Testament the Hebrew word for hope refers to being knitted. We hope because we are firmly knitted into a relationship with the Ultimate Reality.

When Paul writes to Titus about hope, he uses the Greek word *elpis*, which means "to be joyful, confident, welcome." In other words, hope is the joyful confidence by which we welcome the miracles of God. Hope means that we are convinced that God will act in the future as He has acted in the past.

The MVP is on my Squad.

(COOD)

The Apostle Paul would have liked ESPN.

His letters are full of sports metaphors. You know he must have regularly checked out whatever the ancient equivalent was to our sports pages. He wrote about boxing and wrestling, and most of all about running. That's because sports were such a big deal in the ancient world. There were the popular Isthmian Games in Corinth, the Pan-Ionian Games in Ephesus, and, of course, the Olympic Games in Athens. Sports were all the rage in Paul's day.

The foot race was, without question, the most popular event in the ancient *Wide World of Sports*. Every major city had their stadium, where people would crowd in to witness the runners showing their stuff. So, when he wrote his letter to the Christians at Corinth, Paul told them:

> You've been to the stadium and seen the athletes race. A bunch of people line up at the starting line, but only one wins. So run to win. All good athletes train hard. They do it for the gold medal, but that gold medal eventually tarnishes and fades. What you are after is the one that is gold eternally. I don't know about you, but

I am running hard for the finish line. I'm giving it everything I've got (the Authorized Ben Courson Translation).

Can't you just imagine Paul running with abandon, his legs churning and his chest straining toward the tape? He ran like winning this race was everything. Because for him…it was.

When I was in seventh grade, I joined the track team. One of the races I participated in was the 400-meter dash. It was brutal, and honestly, I hated every second of it. After all, it's like running a long-distance sprint.

And I had my issues as a runner. A lot of the problem arose from my tendency to keep glancing backward to see who was behind me. And every time I glanced back I lost some of my momentum. You have to stay focused on the goal if you are going to win the race. Looking back is disastrous. You have to keep moving forward.

And the really dumb part? I wasn't that good of a runner, so when I glanced back over my shoulder it looked like the rapture had taken place behind me.

When Paul wrote to the Philippians, he said that he was forgetting what was behind him and reaching for the prize of the upward calling of God.

Paul said he had stopped looking back. Instead, he was laser focused on the trophy that awaited the first across the finish line.

My Squad of Optimisfits and I try to maintain that same kind of focus. We call that focus *hope*.

We leave the past in the dust. We forget about what is behind us. We put the pedal to the metal. The past sees only our taillights.

Hebrews says that we are to run the race set before us with endurance, keeping our eyes on the author and finisher of our faith. In the ancient world the trophy was usually placed right there at the finish line, so that you could fix your eyes on it as you ran your race. It was the most effective kind of motivation. When your feet started to feel heavy or you began to run out of breath, you could just raise your eyes to the prize and find a fresh burst of energy.

The author of Hebrews goes on to encourage us to lay aside all the burdens that might encumber our progress. Anything that weighs us down needs to be cast aside. Runners don't keep their warm-up clothes on when it's time to race. No, they strip down to lightest-weight gear. The ancient Greeks took this principle so literally that they competed in the nude. The 100-yard dash in the buff.

Talk about running free…

Our hope gives us the focus to do the hard work of running well.

My friend Will, who is a professional soccer player, says that you earn your trophies at practice; you just pick them up at the competition.

That is the kind of confidence we live with.

That is the kind of hope that fuels our race.

22

SOMETHING WORTH DYING FOR

My friend Peter Unger is about as Germanic as they come.

Blond hair. Blue eyes. Strong Germanic name that probably should have an umlaut over the letter *u*. Physically, he looks like Hitler's dream of the perfect human specimen.

Years ago, he decided he didn't want to be a cog in the white-collar corporate system. He wanted to *live* for a living. Now he has become a poster child for Generation Z neo-entrepreneurship.

He's a little like Jay Z, who said: "I'm not a businessman; I'm a business, man."

Autonomy is his jam.

For Peter, life isn't about having two-point-five kids, a dog named Spot, and a white picket fence. It's about more than working 40 hours a week for 40 years so that you can retire on 40 percent of your income, get your 401K and a timeshare in Palm Springs, tool around in your golf cart for a few years, and then claim your spot in the cemetery.

To Peter, the classic American Dream sounds more like a nightmare.

And he wants to wake people up.

(((())))

Peter likes to say things that will annoy people.

On the Fourth of July, when everyone was celebrating how the United States is the land of freedom, he posted this on his Instagram: "We always talk about how we live in America where there's freedom. But most of the world is free. Seventy-five percent of the world is free. America is one of 146 countries that are free. Happy Fourth!"

Yeah. That kind of thing.

He likes to speak truth to power, as they say. He really hates the System. And he hates all the neat little assumptions about God and country.

One day he started talking to me about how Rockefeller and Carnegie set up the American educational system to create docile slaves for the modern industrial revolution. Not sure about the accuracy of that, but it does make my point—he is no fan of the corporate state.

Peter doesn't want to be controlled by anyone.

Not by corporate America.

Not by the political system.

Not by the church.

Peter is a subversive, working inside the System only as much as he has to, but always wary of its siren song, and ready to pour a bracing bucket of ice-cold water over people's assumptions so he can awaken them from the American Dream. Because it isn't a big enough dream.

He has bigger dreams.

He says that if your dreams don't exceed your current capacity to achieve them...they just aren't big enough.

And if your dreams don't scare you...they're not big enough.

⟨⟨⟨⟨⟩⟩⟩⟩

Peter isn't afraid of power.

As George Bernard Shaw once wrote: "Power does not corrupt men; fools, however, if they get into a position of power, corrupt power." That explains a lot about our world today.

Peter has no intention of being a fool.

⟨⟨⟨⟨⟩⟩⟩⟩

Let's face it: There is no such thing as a moderate revolutionary.

If you want to change the world you've got to be extreme. Peter is as extreme as a suicide bomber, but in his case, *he* is the bomb himself—dropped down into a complacent world so that he can explode all the forms of false comfort and get us thinking about the things that really matter. He wants to give his life for a cause that is worth dying for.

Namely: maximum sending.

23

WEAK IS THE NEW STRONG

There are 613 separate laws in the Law of Moses, found in the first five books of the Old Testament. They cover just about any topic you can think of.

When Jesus was asked which was the most important of them, He was ready with an answer. Which in itself is kind of surprising, since when Jesus was asked a question He usually responded by asking a question of His own. This tended to throw the religious leaders off their game.

When He asked them where John got his authority to baptize, "from heaven or from man?" the Pharisees knew that Jesus had impaled them on the horns of a dilemma. If they said that his authority was from man, then they knew the crowds of loyal followers would go ballistic. But if they said it was from heaven, then it was effectively an admission that what John had said about Jesus was true. The best answer they could muster was, "We don't know."

Boom. Game, set, match.

Throughout His ministry Jesus kept the conversation focused where it should be by asking a question of His interlocutors.

But when it came to the question of what was the most critical concern in the Scriptures, Jesus didn't hesitate for a moment to give a straightforward response. Under the full gaze of His piercing eyes, and looking His inquirer full in the face, He told them that everything hinged on love.

Love for God.

Love for our neighbor.

That's the message of Jesus in a nutshell, especially if we add to it His directive to love our enemies. After all, as G.K. Chesterton reminds us, we should love our neighbor and love our enemy…because often they are the same person!

(0000)

If you are living the Optimisfit life, some people just aren't going to like it. You must be prepared to make a few enemies. Winston Churchill was someone who knew what it was like to stand up to opposition. He once said, "You have enemies? Good. It means you stood up for something at some time in your life."

When Churchill was scheduled to speak, the announcement would cause the halls to be filled to overflowing. When he was asked how it made him feel to be able to pack 'em in like that, he smiled his wry smile and answered, "It's quite flattering, until I consider that the halls would be twice as full if they were coming to see me being beheaded."

When you stand up for something that matters to you, you better be prepared to be shouted down sometimes. And when you are, the best response is to love the shouters.

A recent study reported that no matter who you are, 25 percent of the people you meet won't like you. No. Matter. What. Another 25 percent won't like you at first, but might be won over. Another 25 percent like you, but could be persuaded to change their mind. And the last 25 percent are your fan base. They always love you, but keep in mind that this includes your mom, and well, she *has* to like you. It's actually kind of freeing to think about this. No matter what you do, you are not going to get everyone to like you. And even the nicest blokes will have their detractors. So, what do you do? You just take the criticism in stride.

And the harder you work to change the world, the more enemies and naysayers you are likely to gather. Because most people don't want new ideas. They don't want to change or be challenged, thank you very much.

Don't make me feel guilty. Don't make me feel uncomfortable. Don't challenge my ideas or ask me to look at things differently. Just let me stay comfortable believing what I want to believe.

That is the chorus of those who don't want to hear what you have to say and set themselves up as your enemies. They are stubborn.

So, we should be stubborn right back. We should love them stubbornly. They can't keep us from loving them.

Our haters are our motivators.

And since when did tigers lose sleep over the opinions of sheep anyway?

⦅⦆⦆⦆

An entire ocean of water can't sink a ship, unless it gets inside the ship.

All the negativity and criticism can't take us down unless we let it get inside us. No jerk can make me do anything or get a reaction out of me unless I give him permission to get inside my head.

Instead of letting that happen, we can decide to throw love around like confetti.

The same Jesus who was criticized, cursed, spat upon, and nailed to a cross...and who knew this would be His fate told them to love their enemies, to pray for those who use you or curse you or hate you. And when it comes to cheeks, it is always good to turn them.

When the moment came, Jesus practiced the very things He had preached. He loved the very people who had come to execute Him.

Jesus did not come to destroy. He came to save. He chose redemption over destruction.

When the Romans came to arrest Him in the Garden of Gethsemane, He was already sweating drops of blood as He prayed. This was the first time He bled for us. Paul tells us that Jesus is the last Adam. The first Adam was expelled from the Garden of Eden and sentenced to work by the sweat of his brow. Now, the last Adam was back in a garden, bleeding by the sweat of His brow to redeem man's work. It was, you might say, a curse reverse.

There, in the garden—at the crossroads—Jesus chose the road to the cross.

It was the pivotal moment in Jesus' life. He had taught others to love their enemies and pray for those who persecuted them. To bless those who cursed them. To do good to those who hated them. To turn the other cheek. And now, the question was: would He abide by His own teachings? Would He love the very ones who came to execute Him?

Sure enough, Jesus didn't call on a squadron of angels to rescue Him or do battle against His enemies. In fact, when Peter drew his sword to protect Jesus, he was given a stern rebuke.

Jesus accepted the task at hand, He gave Himself freely into the hands of His adversaries, and He walked the lonely road to His crucifixion, even as His friends fled or denied Him.

He went the extra mile for us. And one thing you can say about the path of the extra mile is that it is never crowded.

⟨⟨⟨⟩⟩⟩

There is something very interesting to be gleaned from Jesus' words about turning the other cheek. He said that if someone slaps you on the right cheek, then turn and offer him the left one. Let's think about this for a minute. Most people are right-handed. So, how do you strike a person on his right cheek with your right hand? Well, unless you are some sort of contortionist it means that you slap him with the back of your hand. And in Jewish culture a backhand was considered twice as insulting as being hit with the flat of your hand. You would only back-hand someone of a lower caste in the Jewish hierarchy, such as your slave or servant. To hit someone with the flat of your hand, however, was to admit them as an equal (albeit as an equal that had ticked you off royally).

So, Jesus is saying that if someone backhands you, turn the other cheek so that enemy has to strike you as an equal. Turning the other cheek then, is no sign of weakness. It is a symbol of putting yourself and your enemy on the same footing. It is a choice that takes away the power of the oppressor.

Or if someone asks for your tunic, will you be like St. Francis of Assisi and give away every stitch of clothing, putting aside all your dignity, and stand naked before your enemy? Francis did that literally, as he renounced all his father's riches and re-clothed himself in the simplest of garments. When you see someone naked it makes everyone feel overdressed.

Or, if someone demands you to go one mile, then go the extra one. Since Israel was an occupied territory during the time of Jesus, it gives extra power to this saying. According to Roman law, a Roman could tap a Jew on the shoulder with the flat of his spear and demand that he carry his luggage for him for a mile, just like a beast of burden. But it was against the law for a soldier to demand that he carry it two miles. If he carried it an extra mile, that was technically breaking the law. This is a good reminder that we have the choice as to how we respond to those who wrong us. The extra mile is our choice. It is saying yes to a different way of relating to the one who is making unreasonable demands upon us.

Our choices can disempower the enemy.

Gandhi called it soul-power. When he led the Indian people under British rule in a peaceful protest centered on *not* fighting back, it led the British to relent. They eventually had to sail away from India because Gandhi wouldn't fight back. When Martin Luther King Jr. followed Gandhi's example of nonviolent civil disobedience he could begin the long job of overturning racial injustice in the United States. It didn't come without a price, without some pain and suffering and sacrifice, but change was initiated when the choice was made to turn the other cheek.

Turning the other cheek isn't the sign of being a doormat. It is a sign of strength.

It says that you will not sink to the level of the enemy by engaging in revenge or payback.

Frankly, it annoys our enemies when we don't retaliate with an "eye for an eye" response, because it puts us on the moral high ground.

It annoys our enemies when we won't fight back, because it is intimidating when someone won't play by the usual rules of revenge.

It annoys our enemies when we won't be the aggressor, because it demonstrates that the only kind of aggression with ultimate power is aggressive love.

◯◯◯◯◯

Jesus' love for His enemies was so intimidating that it made them rethink their actions and change their minds, like the Roman soldier who looked on at the crucifixion and figured out what it all meant.

We can be loving, because we have let God love us. We can give out love, because He has given us His love. We can't dispense love if we are drawing from an empty tank. It starts by filling up with His love. As John the Apostle writes in one of his letters, "This is love, not that we loved God, but that He loved us" (1 John 4:10).

◯◯◯◯◯

The world tells us that when we are wronged we should fight back.

But then again, since when did Optimisfits ever obey what we are told we should do? Our act of rebellion is stubborn love.

24

ON GOD'S BEAT

I've long been a fan of the Beat Poets, those freewheeling writers who traveled around the United States in the '50s and wrote fiery, passionate prose about what they thought and experienced. I remember being blown away by reading *On the Road*, the story of the crazy, chaotic, poetic journeys of Jack Kerouac, Neal Cassady, and their compatriots. I wasn't exactly stoked about their experiments with drugs and free sex, but I loved their passionate rebellion against conformity. They weren't interested in fitting in, playing it safe, or chasing our culture's idea of the successful life. Instead, they just wanted to live with maximum passion.

Kerouac writes about his own Squad, and says that they "never yawn or say a commonplace thing." Rather, they "burn, burn, burn like fabulous yellow roman candles exploding like spiders across the stars."

He recorded the whole book on a roll of butcher paper, scribbling away while Cassady took the wheel, careening across the wide landscape of America in search of a different way to approach life. His poetic jottings inspire me to think about finding a better way to walk the Jesus path.

My own Squad of Optimisfits has taken them on as a sort of model for our lives. In many ways, I like to think our way of living is an answer to what was best in the Beat Poets.

They dropped acid. We are high on life.

They listened to jazz. We frequent EDM raves.

They read Dostoyevsky. We can't get enough of George MacDonald.

They lived "on the road." We save our money and head to Iceland. Just because we can.

They proved they were modern cowboys by breaking the rules of grammar, such as putting periods in. random. places. We break the rules of conformity. Period.

Breaking rules is where you find life.

Jesus was the greatest rule breaker of all time. The God-in-the-flesh, beat-poet-of-existence, rebel-lover rule breaker. He broke rules all the time. He never seemed to worry too much about what the pious Pharisees were expecting of Him. He stood up to them and called them on the way they had made life about rules rather than a wild adventure with God.

The religious people of His day were more worried about breaking the letter of the Law than they were about people. Since the Law of Moses said that you couldn't bear a burden on the Sabbath, they started dissecting exactly what that might mean. They actually debated whether a father could lift his child on the Sabbath, if a woman could wear a wig, if the elderly could wear their dentures, or if a maimed person could strap on their wooden limb. After all, each of these might technically be considered "burdens" that were being carried. And if you were a doctor you would be breaking the Sabbath to treat a patient unless the disease was life threatening.

Talk about straining at a gnat and swallowing a camel.

So, what does Jesus do as He wanders about Israel preaching and teaching? He heals people on the Sabbath. In the Gospels He does this seven times. This is against the Law of the Sabbath. Does He care about the Sabbath? Yes, but not as much as He cares about people.

I want to be like Jesus when I grow up.

Which is to say, I want to be rebellious against all the rules and conformity.

⬭⬭⬭⬭

The older generation tells us to grow up.

We just say, "No thanks." We aren't that interested in making them feel comfortable. We are interested in making a difference. We aren't dope dealers. We are hope dealers.

Researchers tell us the average child laughs 200 to 400 times a day. The average adult, on the other hand, laughs between thirteen to seventeen times a day. What?!

I think if you aren't laughing a lot, you really aren't paying attention.

Seriously.

A VERY PROFOUND STATEMENT

If you want to be number one, you have to be odd.

Just sayin'…

WHAT SHERLOCK HOLMES TAUGHT ME ABOUT MY ATTIC

Some people just make life so difficult.

Not long ago I had someone pull me aside to let me know he had a burden on his heart that he wanted to share with me. I readied myself to hear what heavy truth he was feeling compelled to share. His heavy truth was that he thought I spent too much time skateboarding.

Seriously?

Such people don't keep their unhappiness to themselves. They seem set on making everyone else's life difficult too. In the words of John Green, they maintain their lovely figures by eating nothing but the souls of kittens and the dreams of impoverished children.

These curmudgeons come in two varieties: the secular variety and the religious variety. But in either case they are the stone-faced mortal enemies of those of us who think life should be fun. They are sour-faced atheists who want to drain every drop of mystery out of the world. They are bitter, twisted, hurting people who want to make sure that everyone is as miserable as they are. Or they are old-fashioned worshippers of the System—legalists and fanatical religious wet blankets. What both varieties have in common is that those of us who are Optimisfits make them extremely uncomfortable. They'd like nothing more than to make us see "reality" and feel a little worse about it.

But Optimisfits think that reality is more like a dream than a nightmare.

We've learned that the worst way to respond to these people is to get all twisted out of shape about their lack of understanding. A curmudgeonly Optimisfit is a contradiction in terms. How can we be childishly optimistic if we are all angry and bitter toward those who don't have a clue about the way we see life?

So, in a world where there are a lot of ignorant legalists running around doing and saying awful things, draining the joy and adventure out of life, and either denying the reality of God or treating Him like a Cosmic Policeman, how do we not let that affect us?

Let us inquire of the ultimate problem solver: Sherlock Holmes.

◯◯◯◯◯

In the nineteenth century, Arthur Conan Doyle wrote a series of novels and short stories about a detective named Sherlock Holmes and his sidekick, Dr. Watson. They were an almost instant hit with British and American readers. People couldn't get enough of these stories. Except for Doyle himself, who eventually tired of writing about Holmes and wanted to write something else. So, Doyle crafted a story in which Holmes and his arch-nemesis Moriarty are wrestling near the precipice of Reichenbach Falls and then plunge together to their deaths. Done. The End.

Except that Doyle's audience wouldn't hear of it. His readers rose up in outrage and demanded that he bring Sherlock back. One chap spotted Doyle walking down the street and actually beat him up for killing off his hero. Doyle's own mother wrote him an indignant letter, castigating him for even considering such a thing. "Kill that nice Mr. Sherlock Holmes? Foolishness. Don't you dare!"

So, Doyle contrived a semi-plausible explanation for the "apparent" death of Holmes and relaunched the series.

I'm glad that Sherlock came back from the dead. I always admired his style and his methods in solving crimes. No puzzle was beyond his intellect. So, what was his secret?

Well, in the very first Holmes novel, *A Study in Scarlet*, the awestruck Watson finds himself amazed by the breadth of the great detective's knowledge. Only later does he realize that there are some pretty significant gaps in Holmes' knowledge. How could such a genius problem solver not know, for example, that the earth revolved around the sun?

Holmes said that it was all about focus:

> I consider that a man's brain originally is like a little empty attic, and you have to stock it with such furniture as you choose. A fool takes in all the lumber of every sort that he comes across, so that the knowledge which might be useful to him gets crowded out, or at best is jumbled up with a lot of other things so that he has a difficulty in laying his hands upon it. Now the skillful workman is very careful indeed as to what he takes into his brain-attic. He will have nothing but the tools which may help him in doing his work, but of these he has a large assortment, and all in the most perfect order. It is a mistake to think that that little room has elastic walls and can distend to any extent. Depend on it, there comes a time when for every addition of knowledge you forget something that you knew before. It is of the highest importance, therefore, not to have useless facts elbowing out the useful ones.[6]

It's focus, people. Focus.

You heard it from Sherlock himself. Anything that didn't help him solve crimes had no place in his brain. The mind is like an attic, and if you fill it with rubbish it's hard to get at the useful stuff.

That's why an Optimisfit is careful about what we put into our brain. We can't afford to clutter it with junk. There's no room for bitterness or grudges. We won't let un-forgiveness have the run of the place. Scientists tell us that we have over 30,000 thoughts a day, and we aren't going to waste any of them on nursing grievances and keeping score of slights.

We have more important stuff to do. More important stuff to fill our brains with.

To start with, we are too busy to waste time on negativity. We have footballs to catch while skateboarding, and books by Chesterton that need reading. Why spoil the fun by reopening old wounds and poring over our disappointments?

Sure, we will be wronged by others. But why not just *fuggetaboutit*? Why not keep the attic clear of unnecessary negative emotional clutter?

◦◦◦◦

The Apostle Paul tried to tell us way back in the first century: "Love keeps no record of wrongs." That is still good advice. In the Greek language the word for "record" was an accounting term that meant registering an item in a ledger. What Paul was getting at is that the quickest way to kill love (and kill your fun) is to keep a running tally of the evils that have been perpetrated against you.

Frankly, bitterness is for chumps.

Optimisfits have no intention of being chumps because 1) we'd rather pet giraffes, and 2) there are skateboards to kick flip, and 3) there is a world to conquer, which 4) can't be done if we are sitting in our rooms licking our wounds, so yeah 5) we prefer to live the dream…thank you very much.

So just get over it.

Otherwise all the fun will keep getting sapped out of your life.

We have been forgiven. We need to forgive.

As Elsa from *Frozen* sings, "Let it go."

(XXXX)

As is so often the case, Jesus had the perfect story to get us thinking straight about forgiveness. There was once this master who forgave his servant 10,000 talents (that's a lot of money in ancient near-Eastern financial terms). In fact, someone has calculated that if you were to break this much money into coins that it would require an army of 8,600 men, each carrying a 60-pound sack, forming a line five miles long to carry it. But this servant had a fellow who owed him a trifling 100 denarii (that's not much more than Taco Bell meal money—literally *pocket change*). Fresh off being forgiven his own debt he shows up at this other dude's door and demands his 100 denarii. He threatens him with legal action. This man had a Bill Gates-sized debt, yet he wouldn't forgive the pocket change. Of course, the master was furious.

When we consider the forgiveness that God has extended to us, we should realize that we have no right to demand recompense for the pocket change worth of grievances done toward us by others.

Toss the ledger in the mental garbage pail. No need to carry that around, or store it in the mental attic.

(XXXX)

All fine and good, some cynics might say. Easy for you to talk about forgiveness. You don't know what it's like to be betrayed.

Actually, I know exactly what it feels like.

It's terrible to get lied to and cheated on. It is awful to be stabbed in the back and abandoned by people you love. It's no fun to be gossiped about or turned on or ripped off in a business venture. Like you, I've been hurt by people. Not in an abstract sense either. Really.

Everyone on the Jesus path is going to have to deal with a deep wound like this at some point. It's part of living on the planet. There is always a Judas waiting to turn you over to your enemies…after he lays a kiss on you.

Do we turn bitter, or do we grow through what we go through?

When we stand at the crossroads, an Optimisfit chooses the way of the cross.

We'll all be a lot happier if we learn to forgive one another. "Blessed," said Jesus, "are the merciful." According to research from the Mayo Clinic, letting go of grudges can make way for greater happiness, health, and peace. It can lead to lower blood pressure, a stronger immune system, and improved heart health. Showing mercy to others can even help our bodies fight off sickness.

Lewis Smedes once wrote, "To forgive is to set a prisoner free and discover the prisoner was you."

How much un-forgiveness are you packing around? Enough to fit in a wallet? A backpack? Or would it take a wheelbarrow? In any case, do you really want to be hauling that baggage around everywhere you go? Or stuff it into your already crowded mental attic?

Just let it go.

27

JUST SHOOT

If I had been at Columbine and the shooter had looked me in the eye and said, "I'm gonna kill you if you're a Christian. Are you a Christian?" I might have to hem and haw and respond, "Well…it's complicated."

When you talk about the *religion* of Christianity you are bringing in all the baggage of the Crusades and the Witch Trials and the wars between Protestants and Catholics and the wars between Protestants and other Protestants and the crooked TV evangelists and the people who sell salvation like it was an Amway product and the talking heads who confuse faith with political agendas and the hypocrites and the phonies and all the various smug and self-righteous zealots.

Yes, it is complicated.

But if the same gunman looked me in the eye and said, "I'm gonna kill you if you are a child of God. Are you a child of God?" then I would just smile and say, "Yes. Shoot me now."

I would die for a title like that. I would die for Him.

Proudly.

And fearlessly.

28

FRANKL'S SEARCH FOR MEANING

Another of my Optimisfit heroes was a psychoanalyst by the name of Viktor Frankl.

Frankl suffered the full wrath of Auschwitz and Dachau, living through the horror of those Nazi extermination camps, and knowing that any day could be his last. But he managed to survive and live to tell his story. And that almost unimaginably terrible experience made a huge difference in how he thought about life.

On the other side of his experiences in the concentration camp, Frankl developed a theory of psychology that asserted that our primary motivation in life can be found in our search for meaning. He noticed that the people who didn't give up in the camps were the people who kept finding meaning in their lives and a reason to go on. Those that didn't find a meaning for their lives mostly gave up the fight and let themselves be crushed by their experience. He argued that we have means, but no meaning, and we have enough to live by, but not enough to live for.

Life, he asserted, was not a quest for pleasure, as Freud had propagated with his obsession about infantile sexuality, Oedipus complexes, and daddy issues. Nor was it a quest for power, as Alfred Adler had proposed. It was a quest for meaning. Therefore, the greatest task for any person is to find meaning in his or her life.

Frankl believed that all of us are hardwired for meaning—that we all need a purpose for our existence. He believed a person could find meaning in work (doing something significant), in love (deeply caring for other people), and in finding courage during difficult times.

Once, while teaching a college course, he opened the time up for questions. One of the students asked him if he could articulate, in a single sentence, the meaning of his own life. Frankl took a piece of paper and jotted down one brief sentence. Then he asked his students to guess what he had written.

After a few quiet moments of uncomfortable silence, one student raised his hand and offered this guess: "The meaning of your life is to help others find meaning in theirs."

"Those are the very words I wrote," said Frankl.

He went on to write his most famous book, *Man's Search for Meaning*, in just nine days. It is a book that has helped many people discover that life is not meaningless, but that meaning is made every day by the way we choose to live our lives. It is a book bursting with hope. A hard-earned hope, forged in the crucible of the most horrifying circumstances. It is a reminder that no matter how dark things look, we can always find something beautiful and eternal in their midst.

Suffering, in and of itself, is meaningless. We give our suffering meaning by the way in which we respond to it.

"Man," he wrote, "is that being who invented the gas chambers of Auschwitz; however, he is also that being who entered those gas chambers upright, with the Lord's Prayer or the Shema Israel on his lips."

That's not just some sort of positive thinking. That's fire.

That's the courage of the Optimisfit.

That is our passion to help others find the meaning that will make their lives more than just endurable, it will make their lives sing.

〔〇〇〇〇〕

My dream doesn't change when my circumstances change. We choose our responses. We create them. They don't create us.

The enemy whispers in my ear: "You can't survive the storm."

I whisper back to him, "I am the storm."

29

A CAVEAT

Just to be clear, I'm not setting myself up as some perfect example of how to live.

Believe me, I have my issues. Lots of them.

I've been accused of suffering from OCD. But I have two responses to that. First, I'm not suffering. I just embrace that as part of who I am. And second, if you must label my tendencies, then let's agree that I have CDO, because I am more comfortable with having the letters of the ailment in neat alphabetical order like they are supposed to be.

So…

I was a pretty terrible student in school and I don't have as many degrees as a thermometer behind my name. And I probably have as many IQ points as the Cleveland Browns normally put on the scoreboard.

One of my biggest weaknesses is the problem I have had with anger. When I get mad, I tend to get really mad and say and do things I am not proud of later. I'm not halfway with anything, including anger.

Want to make something of that?!

In high-school basketball I led the league in technical fouls. I was John McEnroe when the call went against me, arguing and stomping around and punching the wall.

This is made even more embarrassing because my team was the only Christian school in the conference. Great example I was setting, huh?

I'm not going to make excuses. I take all this seriously, and I am doing the work I need to do to change. I'm getting there, even if a little slowly. The good news is that God has been able to use me in so many ways despite these—and other—imperfections.

The thing that causes me to flare up in anger so easily is probably related to the thing that makes me passionate and driven. I just need to figure out how to make sure I am using my emotion in a healthy way.

Thankfully, I have a Squad walking alongside me through life that is not afraid to keep me honest. They know how to defuse my occasional anger with a good dose of loving ridicule. I get mad and they laugh at me. It's kind of amazing how laughter totally takes all the wind out of anger.

⊙⊙⊙⊙

But really, could we just rename my condition as CDO?

I'd feel better about that.

30

THE UNEDITED ME

My friends have a lot to put up with in me.

I have an unfortunate tendency to act a little cocky or overly self-confident. Sometimes I am a poor listener and too anxious to get my thoughts expressed rather than giving an ear to others. I am impatient with people I find boring or who give off a religious vibe. If you aren't real around me I may react in a way that isn't too kind. And my impatience with others—and often with myself—leads me to struggle with getting angry a little too quickly and a little too passionately.

These are some of the flaws that—for better or worse—make me who I am.

One of the things that religious people are worried about is looking good for their religious peers. To gain respect in the religious world often means demonstrating that you are a better Christian than any of the other Christians; in short, that you are good at following the rules and living up to the expectations. You don't have to be a believer very long to catch on to what you need to do and say if you want to be thought of as a good Christian.

Of course, that means, among other things, covering up who you really are. Keeping your faults well hidden. I mean, you can show some insignificant faults, but make sure nobody sees your deep struggles and failings, the things you battle against nearly every day that make you feel like you aren't making much progress. Keeping the real you out of sight.

Perception is reality in the religious world, so you need to maintain the façade.

Which frankly, I have learned is *way* more trouble than it is worth.

Of course, it isn't just religious people who are overly focused on image—on creating a perception of *who* you are that isn't really based in reality. Where would social media be if it weren't such a powerful tool for creating an idealized image of *who* each of us are? On Facebook and Twitter and Instagram we can carefully construct an image of who we want people to think we are by carefully choosing just the right pictures (probably digitally enhanced), videos, well-thought out and cleverly constructed statements, and posts that show we are hip and cool and interesting…and that our lives are better than most people's lives.

It's all just a big game. And it takes way too much energy to keep it going.

So, I'm just going to try to be myself—warts and all—and accept that some people won't find me acceptable.

I have lots of flaws.

I've tried to be as honest as I could in this book. I wanted you to see the unedited version of me.

And I take comfort in Paul's words, "If I must boast I will boast of the things that show my weakness" (2 Corinthians 11:30 NIV).

Here is where I take great hope. I am not the sum of my flaws and failings. I can choose to see myself as God—who sees me better and more fully than anyone—sees me.

According to the Bible, I am light. I am a temple for the Holy Spirit. I am a citizen of Heaven. I am seated in heavenly places. I am His workmanship, His masterpiece, His poem. I am the pearl of great price that the Master of Heaven would bankrupt His Kingdom to buy.

Where I am weak, He is strong.

That is who I am.

⟨⟨⟨⟨⟩⟩⟩⟩

I refuse to let other people define who I am or what I should do or how I should think.

Proverbs 29:25 tells us that the fear of man is a snare. Worrying too much about what others think will trap you. It is inevitable that some people aren't going to like you. The people who applaud your coronation might well be the same people who applaud your execution.

Many of the same people shouting "Hosanna" when Jesus made His triumphal entry into Jerusalem would a week later be crying out, "Crucify Him!"

In Acts 14, Paul healed a guy in Lystra who had been paralyzed from birth, and the people responded by calling him a god. Shortly thereafter, the people of Lystra stoned him.

Which all goes to say: Don't trust your self-confidence to the poll data.

⟨⟨⟨⟨⟩⟩⟩⟩

I love my friends, but they aren't going to define me either. I am defined by who I am when I am alone with the God who loves me. He is my Abba. My Heavenly Daddy. When I feel like I need some more self-confidence I can always climb up into His lap and He gives me something better: *God*fidence.

(((((

Ralph Waldo Emerson:

> When a resolute young fellow steps up to the great bully, the world, and takes him boldly by the beard, he is often surprised to find it comes off in his hand, and that it was only tied on to scare away the timid adventurers.[7]

Retreating from the expectations of others doesn't mean that you are going to end up living alone as a hermit or a crazy cat lady. In fact, it makes you less likely to end up alone. You become more attractive to people because you aren't so clingy with them, not so dependent upon them, not always trying to get their attention. Instead, you can love them from the place of being comfortable with who you are. And that frees them to be more comfortable with who they are.

Everybody wins.

So, remember: People are not your dictionary. They don't define you.

31

JELLYFISH

O death, where is your sting?

Well, it could be in the stinger of a jellyfish.

I remember when a bunch of us in my Squad were in the south of France, spending the night sleeping on the warm, white beach of the Mediterranean Sea. We woke up with our faces caked in sand to the sound of a bird making a whooping sound out at sea. When we looked more closely, that bird seemed to be *standing* on the water itself, as though it were contemplating the limits of physics and deciding it didn't need to be hemmed in by them.

We brushed the sand off our clothes and ran down to the surf, where we plunged in and started doing backflips.

We were laughing hysterically when suddenly my buddy Sean stepped on a jellyfish and it stung him on the foot.

His response? He just started laughing uncontrollably.

"Sean," I said, "that could be dangerous. You might die."

"Well then, I might as well enjoy my last hour of life," he returned.

Solomon was undoubtedly onto something when he said, "A merry heart does good like medicine." Because Sean is alive and kicking—and still grinning at the abyss.

An Optimisfit isn't afraid of dying. We just aren't planning on doing it anytime soon. Until our number comes up, we are going to live at full throttle.

Sean knows the balance. He loves life. But he also has his head in the clouds.

Whenever a plane flies overhead, he brings his skateboard to a stop and turns his eyes to the sky. The sight gets him so excited that he dances a merry jig and his floppy hair goes flying. I guess that's why he has decided to become a pilot. He has adopted the philosophy of Leonardo da Vinci: "When once you have tasted flight, you will forever walk the earth with your eyes turned skyward, for there you have been, and there you will always long to return."

The sting of death is softened when you know that there is something beyond it.

Someday Sean will move into his heavenly mansion.

But not yet.

There is still important laughing that needs to be done.

32

LAUGHING AT FEAR

Sean was all giggles when he got stung by a jellyfish. He thought it was funny.

Crazy, huh?

Honestly, that's just the way he rolls. Whenever Sean gets stressed, he cracks up. In a situation where most people would throw a temper tantrum or freeze like a deer in the headlights, Sean just busts out in uncontrollable laughter.

Scientists tell us that laughing releases neuropeptides in the body, which strengthen the immune system. So my theory is that Sean literally laughed himself to health. It can be proven that depressed people get colds more frequently than the nondepressed, and that people who laugh more often live significantly longer. In fact, laughing a hundred times has the same effect on the body as working out on a rowing machine for ten minutes or on a stationary bike for fifteen.

An hour later Sean was fine.

I'm learning something valuable from him. Just don't take fear so seriously.

A few weeks ago, I told the story about Sean and the jellyfish to an audience, and you could tell they were enjoying it by all the laughter. After the event broke up it was dark and I couldn't see very well. But that didn't stop me, and some of my friends, from grabbing our longboards for a little action. I went bombing down the hill, using my iPhone as a flashlight, and cranking up the EDM. I kept picking up more speed at each turn until I finally lost control and pitched myself onto the cement, tumbling head over heels and finding myself lying on the roadway with blood emerging from several different places on my body. My Squad took me to the emergency room, where I was fitted with a stylish cast and a sling for my arm.

When my friends surveyed the damage and realized I wasn't dead, they smirked, "So, are you gonna laugh like Sean?"

Even though I was in a world of pain, and the blood was still fresh and abundant…I did.

Truth is, laughing really did make me feel better.

Though I still had to give my next talk wearing that sling.

◯◯◯◯

Optmisfits take a whole lot more things a whole lot less seriously.

We defang the dark by laughing in its face.

As Sean's brother Cam says, "I used to be afraid of the dark, but now the dark is afraid of me." Or as Anakin learns in Matthew Stover's *Revenge of the Sith*, "It is not the power of darkness that is to be feared, it is fear that gives power to the darkness."

Maybe that is why you'll find the phrase "fear not" more than two hundred times in the Bible. It is the most frequently repeated commandment in Scripture.

Fear is one of the most debilitating emotions you can experience. It will rob all your joy and confidence and happiness. It will make you respond in all kinds of unhealthy ways, stoking anger and bitterness, and keeping you from experiencing peace.

Just as laughing is good for your health, fear and stress and anger are slowly killing you.

Two of the most common diseases of modern life—the stomach ulcer and coronary thrombosis—are often the direct result of stress and fear. The way we think, doctors tell us, is the root of over 75 percent of the illnesses we experience. Until we get our way of thinking corrected, our reactions to life's experiences may do more damage than the negative experiences themselves.

Laughter, the old saying goes, is the best medicine. Even before that old saying developed, Proverbs 17:22 told us that a merry heart is good medicine.

Are you getting your minimal daily requirement of mirth?

◌◌◌◌◌

Cam once told me, "When fear visits the world, people tremble. And when fear visits the God in us, we crack up."

Laughter is a sign of hopefulness. A sign that you aren't taking the darkness more seriously than it deserves. I love to hear Cam give a talk, because he often must pause midway through his speeches because he can't stop laughing at his own profound thoughts.

Cam is one of the least fearful people I've ever met.

And one of the most hopeful.

He takes life as it comes, without fear, and with tons of hope.

He taught me that any thought in my mind that doesn't inspire hope isn't from God. He never makes fun of me—no matter how much I might deserve it—and he always reminds me of how cool it is that I am created in God's image. How can that not inspire hope?

Zero fear. That is our motto, and the motto of our entire Squad.

Which frees us up to live the adventure. Which we are doing. In spades. We believe that anything worth doing is worth overdoing. We are going to send it. Every time. Period. Even with people who don't vibe with our tribe. Hey, they'll come around.

The world was never changed by vanilla-flavored heroes.

The world is changed by those who dare and dare and dare and dare again—and who know the Great Enthusiasm.

⌒⌒⌒⌒⌒

I first got to know Cam when we rented one of those soccer-mom-style minivans for a road trip so that we could film some scenes for our TV show. Not long into the trip, one of the doors fell off. Being expert mechanics, we did the only sensible thing. We duct-taped it back on.

And on with the show.

Cam and I have never watched a movie together. We've been too busy *living* movies to watch them.

He's the kind of guy who will gaze upon a Taco Bell burrito in the last glow of daylight as though it were a sacred object. Or pray for my healing when I have one of those skating mishaps. Or sometimes just sit quietly with me as we listen to the water plunge over a waterfall in the woods at night, basking in the love of God.

Once, on one of our woodland adventures, I had a scorpion jump onto my arm. My first thought was panic, but Cam just looked at me serenely and I could read the words in his expression: "That scorpion has zero power over you." So, I brushed it off before it could kill me. Zero fear.

Our world is changed by those who refuse to be afraid. Martin Luther. Copernicus. Galileo. Socrates. Steve Jobs. Like them, we can throw back our heads and laugh uproariously at everything fear puts in our way.

"Perfect love," writes the Apostle John, "casts out fear" (1 John 4:18 ESV).

"God has not given us," chimes in the Apostle Paul, "a spirit of fear" (2 Timothy 1:7 CSB). It just isn't who we are when we are children of God.

Love and fear are like matter and antimatter. They can't exist in the same place. One cancels out the other.

Does this all sound too optimistic to you? Perhaps that is just because you haven't tried it. Embracing this kind of attitude changes everything in your personal world. And that empowers you to change the world around you.

The boldest guy in the Old Testament was probably David. He was a fearsome warrior. He used potential fear as fuel. He was a guy who came face-to-face with an adversary who was literally a giant. A *really* big dude. Everyone else quaked in their boots, but he *ran* out to meet him and dispatched a single well-aimed stone from his slingshot and brought the giant down. David was mighty in battle, wielding his sword to slay hundreds of enemy combatants. He even tangled with lions and bears. He wrote in his journal: "I will not be afraid of tens of thousands of people, that have set themselves against me round about" (Psalm 3:6 KJV).

Now we're talking!

(((((())))))

If you want to defeat your fears, you don't have to *do* anything. You just need to let God love you, for when you recognize how deep His love goes, you'll find that fear must vanish in the face of such overwhelming love.

Our part is to jump so that He can catch us.

(((((())))))

Ralph Waldo Emerson said that the person who isn't conquering some new fear every day has not learned the secret of life. We should always be doing the things that we are afraid to do.

In the Bible, God challenged people to not only face their fears, but to *faith* their fears.

What was the prophet Isaiah most afraid of? Public speaking. He had no confidence in his power to craft the right words and deliver them with style. And what did God call him to do? Preach. And to make it even more uncomfortable, He once even asked him to preach naked. God asked him to bare his soul, and to bare his body while he was at it. This man with minimal self-confidence ended up writing the book of the Bible that most scholars consider one of the most beautiful and poetic. But first he had to face the fear.

Shadrach, Meshach, and Abednego were three Hebrew teenagers who had been displaced by the Babylonian captivity. A very long way from their home they didn't do the expected thing. They didn't try to fit in with the customs of the land where they now found themselves. They were not men of convenience, but men of conviction. When they were cast into a fiery furnace for refusing to bend the knee to the religious expectations of a pagan king, they did not shrink from the flames. And the God who is a consuming fire—who never burns what we are, but only what we are not—redeemed them from their fiery tribulation. The flames did not burn them. The flames forged them. In the midst of the attempted roasting they lifted their voices to praise God. I'm willing to bet that they had a good chuckle at the whole situation.

Daniel was another fearless figure. When he was tossed into a den of lions as punishment for praying to the One True God, he just lay down and took a nap among those ferocious felines. Zero fear. Sure deliverance. Daniel was so fearless that he could sleep in a lion's den even though the king was so scared that he couldn't fall asleep in a palace!

Speaking of naps, can you and I be like Jesus, who slept soundly in a boat that was being tossed about wildly by the churning waves? His disciples were in a panic.

Jesus was taking a nap.

(((O)))

When a group of 50 people over the age of 90 were asked what they would do differently if they could live their lives all over again from the start, one of the most common answers was: *I wish I had taken more risks.*

When I'm older I don't want to be found complaining about the cramps I got from playing bingo or shuffleboard. I want to be barreling down the hill on my longboard, even if I've got a touch of arthritis.

I want to be like Yoda, warding off Count Dooku with my geezer stick at nine hundred years old.

I want to be like Caleb, a biblical character who didn't let age slow him down. He didn't retire at a beachside condo in Galilee. Instead, at age 85, he was fighting the Anakim giants. He may have had snow on his rooftop, but he still had fire in his furnace.

I want to be like my grandfather. He was a little crazy, but in the best possible way. I remember visiting my grandparents in their home in the woods when I was a kid. I was out in the yard with my grandma and everything was pretty quiet except for the sound of the birds singing. Suddenly, there was the loud rasping sound of an engine revving up. I must have flinched, because Grandma said, "Don't worry. It's just your grandfather."

Sure enough, my grandpa came roaring down the hill on his dirt bike. He picked up speed as he got closer, went up a little ramp he had built, and proceeded to soar over the top of my mom's VW van. Without a word he turned the bike around and rode away.

If my back is a little sore when I hit 75 years old, I want it to be because I just tried a double backflip on my dirt bike.

I want to be like the palm tree in Psalm 92, which bears fruit into old age. And its fruit only gets sweeter as it gets older.

⟩⟨⟩⟨⟩

In the meantime, I am busy undertaking the quest God has given me. I want to be Luke Skywalker, Katniss Everdeen, Achilles, and Frodo all rolled into one.

More than that, I want to be like Jesus.

Jesus knew what was coming as He slowly made His way to the cross. He could have adjusted His message to make folks more comfortable with it, or forged some helpful alliances with the religious establishment, or hired a group of bodyguards to replace the cowardly disciples. But Jesus showed no fear. Sure, there was a moment of hesitation in Gethsemane, but He knew what needed to be done. And He did it.

I want be like Him.

I want to do something so scary that if God's not in it, I am doomed to fail. Great things never happen in the comfort zones.

So, as I walk through the valley of the shadow I will fear no evil.

I'll live even if the jellyfish stings me. I'll brush off the scorpions. I'll send fear scampering away in terror.

33

MAN ON THE MOUNTAIN

During the Civil War, Ulysses S. Grant was a respected general, so respected that he would eventually become president of the United States. His success as a military leader was founded upon his fearlessness.

One day he climbed alone to the top of a mountain to scout the terrain. But what he saw made his heart beat faster. There were thousands of enemy troops led by General Harrison, and they were preparing for an imminent attack. A wave of fear passed over him.

As his mind raced through the possibilities of how to respond to this overwhelming force, he watched Harrison gather his soldiers into formation...and then begin a hasty retreat. Evidently the very sight of Grant had struck fear into his opposition.

Grant learned something that day that he would never forget: Every one of his adversaries "knows my name, and they are more afraid of me than I am of them."

The enemy of our souls, that wily snake, is more afraid of you than you are of him. For "greater is he that is in you, than he that is in the world" (1 John 4:4 KJV).

Know your God.

And have no fear.

Know your limitations.

And then defy them.

34

THE REBEL JESUS

Gentle Jesus, meek and mild?

Not so much. He overturned the tables of orthodoxy, disrupted the religious system and its ceremonies, taught subversive ideas, and questioned the authority of those who were in power.

One man pitted against the assembled might of Jewish orthodoxy.

Everything He did was a slap in the face of the System.

Everything He did was a deliberate act against Religion.

He talked to women...even prostitutes. That just wasn't done. What about your reputation, Jesus? What will people think?

He ignored the nitpicky regulations of Sabbath—rubbing grain between His hands on the holy day, therefore "harvesting" illegally. What about your reputation, Jesus? What will people think?

He walked into the temple area and angrily overturned the tables at which the moneychangers sat; they were just trying to keep the sacrificial system going according to the rules. What about your reputation, Jesus? What will people think?

He didn't care what people thought. Especially what the Pharisees thought.

The fact that some people addressed Him as "Rabboni" probably indicates that Jesus was very possibly a Pharisee Himself, the group of orthodox Jewish leaders who took their faith seriously, but focused more on the outer aspects of religious observance than on having a friendship with Abba. They knew the Bible, but they didn't know God.

If that is true, it means that Jesus was blowing up the System from the *inside*.

⟨⟨⟨⟨⟩⟩⟩⟩

Talk about a misfit. Jesus was definitely someone who was poorly adapted to His environment. He was intent on overturning that environment. And showing us a new way.

⟨⟨⟨⟨⟩⟩⟩⟩

The System is the world as we know it.

The System is religion as we know it.

Diagnosis: The System is broken.

Therefore, torching the System is the only sensible response. Refusing to fit in is the only reasonable reply.

Jesus was killed by the System.

He made everyone uncomfortable—the Roman authorities, the religious Jews, the conditioned masses. He simply didn't fit in. He subverted the very "truths" that the Romans and the Jews were depending on.

He ignored the Laws.

Jesus co-opted the very words that the Romans used for their "peace through strength" message, and offered His own kind of Good News. He waged war through love, forgiveness, and weakness. He stood unafraid before the leaders of the greatest kingdom on earth (the Roman Empire) and said that His only allegiance was to a Kingdom that they could not see.

So, they killed Him. They colluded to take His life, believing that would be the end of His single-minded rebellion against the System.

But burning books and killing rebels only fans the flames.

You can't kill Truth.

And Jesus rose like the phoenix out of those flames.

Jesus is kind of like Sonic the Hedgehog. The Sega system has become extinct, but Sonic remains indestructible. He outlives it, because he is bigger than any system.

⦿⦿⦿

The System that killed Jesus is still with us. It will try to brainwash us into believing that the System is reality.

In the classic film *The Matrix*, Neo was offered the option of swallowing the blue pill and simply accepting the illusions he saw around him as reality, thereby living a life of placid conformity. Or, if he swallowed the red pill he would see things for what they really are.

The Truth.

As Cam once said, "The System is far less an entity to destroy than an illusion to unsee. What keeps the System powerful is the illusion of its power that is engrained in the hearts of the ones whom it seeks to oppress."

Too many Christians have been satisfied with adapting to the System. Of finding a way to comfortably coexist with it.

But a child of God will not accept that option.

We will join the rebellion led by the rebel Jesus.

We take up the weapons of love and wonder to wage a fierce rebellion against hopelessness.

WHAT I LIKE ABOUT RELIGION

Not much.

WHAT I DON'T LIKE ABOUT RELIGION

Pretty much everything.

WHAT THE BIBLE SAYS ABOUT RELIGION

You were included in the death of Christ and have died with Him to the religious system and powers of this world. Don't retreat back to being bullied by the standards and opinions of religion—for example, their strict requirements, "You can't associate with that person!" or, "Don't eat that!" or, "You can't touch that!" These are the doctrines of men and corrupt customs that are worthless to help you spiritually. For though they may appear to possess the promise of wisdom in their submission to God through the deprivation of their physical bodies, it is actually nothing more than empty rules rooted in religious rituals (Colossians 2:20-23 TPT).

Can I get an amen?

38

UNVEILED

The Jewish temple contained a room called the Holy of Holies, which was separated from the rest of the temple by a thick veil. This room was where the presence of God could be experienced in the most intimate way. According to Jewish custom, only the high priest could enter these holy precincts, and when he did, he had to have a rope attached to his foot. That way, if he was struck down by the presence of God, others could haul his body back out without entering themselves.

That is pretty serious stuff.

At the very moment when Jesus died, that temple veil was torn. From the top to the bottom.

Consider that for just a moment. *From the top…to the bottom…* God Himself did the tearing. He destroyed the barrier that was separating Him from human beings.

When He did, it wasn't so much to get us into the presence of God, as to get the presence of God into us. It inaugurated a new kind of intimacy with Him.

In biblical times Jews would rend their garments when they were grieved or deeply shaken by a travesty. Ripping your shirt was a metaphor for rending your heart. It's as if God was so shaken by the barrier separating Him from people that He tore it in grief. So now we can lean on His chest as the beloved disciple did, and hear the very beat of His heart. Tearing the veil, though, was much more than a sign of grief. It was also a sign of victory.

When NFL quarterback Cam Newton scores a touchdown, he tears his jersey in imitation of Superman. So too, Jesus, the Son of Man, triumphantly tore the religious barrier separating Him from the common folk, ripping religion apart forever.

The Old Testament said that we had to take off our shoes when we came upon holy ground. The New Testament says that the Father gives shoes to the prodigal because he's now worthy to stand in Abba's presence as a son.

The Old Testament said that the sheep had to die for the sins of the shepherd. The New Testament says that the Good Shepherd laid down His life for the sins of the sheep.

When the veil was torn, religion was permanently undone.

Because of that, we can know we're kids of the King and friends of God.

How can one even begin to respond to such an amazing truth?

How about...*Woo to the hoo*!

39

NAKED HIPPIES

So, where did my rebellious hopefulness come from?

I can trace the origins of many of my attitudes to my parents.

Mom is one of the most hopeful and positive people on planet Earth. Seriously. She eats rainbow sandwiches for lunch and dines on Pegasus steak. She is drop-dead gorgeous, always happy, and she knows how to make every place feel like it is your long-lost home. She always makes sure the candles are lit, the windows are wide open, and music is drifting in to welcome you. She is a seven on the Enneagram, all about sun and fun. I want to be like her when I grow up. If I ever do…

While my optimism comes from mom, my rebellious side comes directly from my dad. Dad has always loved God passionately, but he never saw much use in religion. He never fit in with the religious establishment. No suits and ties. No strict decorum. He'd preach to the local hippie population who lived in tree houses. Their baptisms were always a wild celebration, because they were baptized naked. No joke. After a particularly effective sermon one day, some of them decided to burn their drugs in a big bonfire to show their repentance. You can imagine the unintended results. High on Jesus, for sure. Another time, while speaking at a Protestant leadership conference, he referred to Catholics as "our brothers and sisters," which caused some 50 pastors to walk out on his talk. He just kept right on preaching his generous and ecumenical message of fellowship and inclusion. It didn't really take him by surprise. He knew exactly what he was doing. If someone didn't think he was adequately pious and orthodox, he could live with that.

So, I'm keeping a positive outlook, but I am also rebelling against conformist religious attitudes. I'm excited about a different way of approaching faith.

⊙⊙⊙

Last night, my friends Cambria and Bo (a.k.a. Cambo) were talking with me about the difference between religion and relationship. Jesus, we agreed, didn't come to set up a new religion. In fact, religion is what killed Him. He didn't want to follow a bunch of nitpicky rules about the Sabbath, for example. Instead He went against the rules and even performed healings on the holy day of rest. People were more important than religious observance.

Pay close attention to the people who made Jesus mad. It wasn't the nonreligious folks. Not the mobsters and call girls. It was the religious leaders; the ones who kept all the rules and regulations, but missed the heart of what Jesus was really all about. He tore down the barriers that kept human beings from experiencing God. He threw the profiteers out of the temple, overturning their tables and overturning the system. He called the Pharisees "sons of the devil." Everything Jesus did was a deliberate act of rebellion against religion. Why else would He purposely try to tick off the religious leaders by telling them they travelled across land and sea to make converts...who then became twice as much the sons of hell as they were. That's cooked.

Sometimes I wonder what would happen if Jesus walked the earth today. Would the pious by-the-book religious leaders hang Him on a cross again for not conforming to their standards, their rules, and their regulations? I think that non-Christians would find Him winsome and fascinating and be hanging on every word, but I wonder if many modern Pharisees would complain that He did unexpected things that made them feel really uncomfortable. Would they start the chorus of "Crucify Him"? I wonder.

Sometimes religion actually turns people away from God. It becomes a substitute for the complexities of a real encounter with God.

Jesus isn't looking for religious commitments out of us. He is offering friendship of the deepest kind.

He created you for the highest of all purposes: *to enjoy the joy of being enjoyed by God.*

That, my friends, is the meaning of life in one sentence.

Bam.

(((((()))))

God's jam isn't getting you to obey more rules—don't drink, don't smoke, don't chew, don't go with girls who do. That wasn't Jesus' message. That is just the religion of Churchianity.

Instead, we are children of God. Being His child is a much more biblical phrase and a much more beautiful reality than is contained in that worn-out descriptor, "Christian." He wants you to be free, to have fun, to enjoy Him to death—His lovingkindness is, the Bible tells us, better than life.

What Cambria and Bo and I decided is that we wouldn't die for religion, but we would proudly die for the One whom Paul calls the "God of Hope." Religion is boring and guilt inducing and conformist. Being God's child, on the other hand, is endlessly exciting. It is the adventure of having a relationship with a wild and surprising God!

Jesus said that He came to deliver the oppressed and set the captives free. Paul tells his readers that "where the Spirit of the Lord is there is freedom" (2 Corinthians 3:17).

You are free.

Free to skate and love and eat Gushers and hang out in hot tubs and talk to God like you would talk to your best friend. Because He is. You are free to laugh and play and watch the stars sparkle against the inky velvet of interstellar space. You are free to live for a living.

Religion is about dealing with your guilt. Relationship is about participating in His glory.

Jesus took a beating on your behalf, so you can stop beating up on yourself.

Religion tells us that we need to convince God to accept us by doing the right things. Relationship tells us that we are accepted already.

God does not endure you. He enjoys you.

God enjoys you so much that He writes songs about you and sings them over you according to Zephaniah 3:17. He thinks you totally rock.

And He should know. He *is* the Rock.

40

THE OPTIMISFIT BLUES

It was still dark when I lifted my iPhone off my nightstand, rubbed my eyes, and mused about how lousy I was feeling. Over the previous days, I had been busy making notes about things I wanted to say in this book, and so I keyed in my unvarnished, honest thoughts.

It was Valentine's Day, and I woke up alone in my bed. My first thought was that I no longer had someone special with whom to celebrate this day. Dark strange thoughts started to swirl in my brain and a deep loneliness descended. I was depressed about girls, and filled with questions about my career as a traveling speaker, and wondering how much I really meant to my friends. I also couldn't help but ponder death, thinking about how I was edging closer to it every day I lived.

⬤⬤⬤⬤

Sometimes it begins to feel like the universe has grown hostile toward my very existence. I am uprooted and drifting, like Camus' Stranger. I can't see hope in this sevenfold horror of outer darkness.

Yes, even an Optimisfit gets the blues now and then.

The worst part for me is feeling alone. When I'm alone with my thoughts, I find that I don't really like the company. There is a reason that solitary confinement is considered the fiercest punishment. I hate being alone in my own head. Valentine's Day isn't much fun for everyone who is unattached. We feel unwanted and we long for some connection. That is what I was feeling when I reached for my iPhone that morning.

What makes it worse is that everyone else seems to be having a great time with the love of their life. All those lovey-dovey Facebook posts and Instagrams. I'm watching their highlight reels about the Beauty of Love and I am stumbling around filled with envy and cynicism.

Like most dudes, it doesn't matter how lost I am...I still don't really want to stop and ask for directions.

⦅⦅⦅⦅⦆

The only cure I have found for this kind of despair is to rethink what Love is really all about.

It isn't just about heart-shaped boxes of chocolates and bouquets of flowers. It isn't just about finding that perfect someone who completes you or at least fills in the loneliness gap.

Because, ultimately, no person can really be the answer for our need for love...except the One who invented it.

The Prime Mover of the universe is Love.

God loves me completely and obsessively. Not for who I *might* be someday, but for who I am today.

Another beloved person might seem to fill the void of our need for love, but it never really holds up. Only He can really fill and fulfill me.

There is no character in any of Nicholas Sparks' romantic novels who loves with the kind of passion that God feels toward me. Romans 8 tells me that nothing can separate me from His love. Nothing.

Not my mistakes. Not my lousy attitudes. Not my repeated failures and doubts. Not the dumb stuff I will probably do about ten minutes from now.

He loves me more than I can possibly understand and more fully than I can possibly feel.

I am the recipient of the greatest love the universe has ever known. And so are you.

That's what every Optimisfit needs to remember on Valentine's Day.

41

900 YEARS YOUNG

Cameron has a pretty basic theme for his life: Every day is an adventure with God.

One time, Cam was in a restaurant and noticed a woman struggling along with a cane. He was so moved with compassion that he offered to pray for her. By the time he left the restaurant with his doggy bag, she didn't need a cane anymore.

So yeah, that happened.

He's the person who taught me that vanilla will never change the world.

He's like a Navy Seal—of the opinion that anything worth doing is worth overdoing.

Once he told me that he was convinced he would live to be 900 years old, and then be translated up to heaven without dying. He had a twinkle in his eye, but I think he was partly serious.

Sounds like a plan.

Cam isn't that interested in watching movies, because he is too busy making his own. He is an amazingly talented videographer and we've worked together to make little movies for my TV show and YouTube. I love the adventure of letting him direct me.

We do jump kicks at the Matterhorn in Switzerland, handstands at the Eiffel Tower, backflips off old dilapidated buildings on the French coast, and skate along Route 66 at 3 a.m., with our path lit only by flares. We go four-wheeling with my Jeep through an old abandoned water park that is filled with graffiti and litter.

You never know what nutty idea he'll come up with next.

But it is always an adventure.

When I asked him, in the words of Mary Oliver, what he planned to do with his one wild and precious life, he shrugged as though the answer was obvious: "World domination with my best friends."

What a world it would be with him in charge.

He loves life. He dances with all the frenzy and wild abandon of King David.

Cam is convinced that part of our mission is to heal the pain, the confusion, and the damage done by this world. He believes what the Bible says about our being seated in "heavenly places," and he wants to harness the power of the world to come and bring it to bear on this one.

He can do this because he sees himself as invincible: "Jesus said I'll never die. I'll take that verse to the bank. I'm gonna live until I'm 900. And that's lowballing it. So, for the millennium or so that I'm alive I'm going to find anything that isn't heaven on earth and utterly destroy it."

That's a pretty straightforward agenda.

Maybe I can read these words at his funeral.

Oh wait.

Maybe we won't really need to have one…

42

PETER PANDEMONIUM

I have another hero that I probably should have mentioned earlier. He doesn't have the intellectual weight of Chesterton and MacDonald, or the fierce zeal of Graham, or the weighty authority of Alexander the Great. (In fact, he is kind of weightless!) But perhaps he adds a nice balance to all those esteemed historical figures, especially since—technically—he isn't real.

His name is Peter Pan.

To many Optimisfits, he is a kind of patron saint. To those who say that life "isn't all fun and games," he reminds us that we'd be better off if our lives *were* more fun and games.

Peter Pan is the fictional creation of author J.M. Barrie, but his way of approaching life is, in many ways, a very real model for me and my Squad.

Peter and his Lost Boys were always up for an adventure. That is our jam too. He reminds us that growing up is for chumps, if growing up means being sucked into the death-in-life program of the white picket fence in suburbia, the all-consuming, ladder-climbing career, and our very own McMansion and two-point-five kids. We think the

American Dream sounds more like a nightmare, and we aren't signing up for that gig.

Instead, we want to turn our everyday lives into Neverland.

That means bucking the System and sticking it to the man. It means thumbing our nose at everyone else's idea about what makes the good life.

In fact, we want to take Peter to the next level: Peter Pandemonium.

⦅⦆⦆⦆

We are ready to be wild emissaries of God's Kingdom. To be anointed with faith and trust and pixie dust.

We want to dance footloose upon this earth, surrounded by other children of God who share a taste for what is joyful, childlike, and anarchistic. We want to shake things. We want to rebel against conformity and normality, and let God do something new in and through us.

We say no to the middle-class nightmare and the rule of the aristocracy.

We say no to Jesus-in-a box and paint-by-number Christianity.

Instead, we are ready for God to use us to shake things up, to ignore the norms, and to reawaken our dreams.

We envision a day when suicide is no longer one of the top ten leading causes of death. We want to usher in a freedom that replaces all the stress and anxiety of trying to conform to the System. It is literally killing people. We want to help people feel more at ease with their inner misfit. Perhaps then all the drugs and counseling won't be quite so urgent. We want to go down in history as the generation that turned things around—that offered people a wild, adventurous, and exciting life of hope.

After all, who made up the rule that we need to assimilate to the hive mind? Why should other people's agendas take precedence over the still small voice within that tells us we are adored just as we are?

The System is broken.

So why submit to a broken System?

Why take ourselves with such deadly seriousness?

Let's recapture a little of the positive chaos of the 1960s. I've seen the television interviews with the Beatles where journalists asked all the serious questions to help viewers put the Fab Four into a neat little box. But John, Paul, George, and Ringo refused to play along. They cracked jokes, fooled around, talked nonsense, and refused to take their interlocutors seriously. No British act had ever gone on television and used it as a forum to goof around. They pioneered a rebellion against the tight-upper-lip Victorian stoicism that you were expected to display in public. They were in open rebellion to the stuffed shirts and the political power brokers and guardians of the normal. So, Ringo took up his drumsticks and they marched to their own beat.

◯◯◯◯

The point is, God isn't looking for us to be good little boys and girls. Jesus isn't a tame lion, and we aren't here to be tamed either.

So, we are ready to be released into something grand and meaningful and, well…fun.

We are the followers of Peter Pandemonium and we are here to rattle the cages, break the locks, and set people free to live as God meant them to. And that ain't a vanilla religious mind-set. It is a call to adventure.

Who the Son sets free is free indeed.

That's why we are raging against hopelessness and telling a new story.

Our story is about the ridiculously prodigal love of God, about beauty, about deep and lasting friendships, and about embracing each day with gleeful abandon and finding the magic and the mystery and the holiness in the ordinary. We are absurdly, uproariously, unapologetically optimistic about the dreams God has given us. He did not put them there to *frustrate* us, but to *fulfill* us!

⟨⟨⟨⟨⟩⟩⟩⟩

Are we Optimisfits safe and predictable? No.

Are we dangerous? I certainly hope so.

⟨⟨⟨⟨⟩⟩⟩⟩

People often think of rebellion as an angry and superserious thing.

Not me and my Squad.

We are total goofballs who understand that changing the world is not only something that should be fun, but that fun is, in fact, the very thing that sets the change in motion. A few minutes ago, I got off the phone with Cam and his brother, Sean. Our conversation essentially consisted of making gorilla noises to each other. These two are brilliant and successful filmmakers, but they know how important it is that work be seasoned with play. And childlike wonder.

That seems like God's way too.

C'mon Peter Pandemonium, Neverland is waiting.

43

AS HUMBLE AS KANYE

Kanye West sends his thoughts into the world via Twitter:

"You may be talented, but you're not Kanye West."

"I wish I had a friend like me."

"Maybe I couldn't be skinny and tall, but I'll settle for being the greatest artist of all time as a consolation."

"I need a room full of mirrors so I can be surrounded by winners."

Ummm. Yeah. No lack of confidence there.

⦾⦾⦾

People who are following God can often show a similar kind of unshakeable confidence.

Think of Moses. Numbers 12:3 tells us that Moses was the most humble man on earth. And you know who wrote that description? Yep. Moses himself, the author of Numbers. And since it is written in the third person it sounds even less convincingly humble. Let's face it. Whether you are an athlete or a rapper or the deliverer of Israel, everything sounds cockier when you refer to yourself in the third person.

But, just to complicate matters, God *told* Moses to write that about himself. And who is going to disagree with God?

⦅⦆

So, I'll take my example from Moses.

I'm gonna say about myself what God says about me.

So, if God tells me that I am made in His likeness, then by golly, I'm not going to be unhappy about what stares back at me from the mirror.

We are His image bearers, crowned with honor and glory, and taking our place alongside the King as His chosen children.

And that is an immortal glory, because we are not just human beings having a spiritual experience; we are spiritual beings that just happen to be having a human experience. Our glory is infinite.

To eternity and beyond!

We should be walking around like we have the cheat codes to win the game of life; like we are Super Mario and have been given the superstar power-up. Death has been undone, so we are claiming our spot in the victor's circle. There is a throne awaiting. Just my size.

Come to think of it, Kanye's boasts seem pretty tame compared to what I can boast as a child of God.

Kanye is confident, but we can be *Godfident*.

Not because of *who* we are, but because of *whose* we are.

We are invincible.

We have bulletproof souls. We can be killed, but we never die.

(((())))

That, my friends, is what Optimisfits like to call hope.

I've given my life to spreading the message of hope. If hope were an Olympic event, I'd be a serious contender for the gold. It's what drives me to climb aboard planes and travel around the globe with this good news about hope.

If you have the best message ever—and we do—then you gotta share it.

If you don't feel a similar compulsion, then perhaps you haven't really understood how big this hope is and the kind of dreams it releases.

You gotta dream a little bigger, darling. And you can, because our dreams are based upon a firm foundation of hope.

Psalm 20:4 says, "May He give you the desire of your heart."

Psalm 145:19 promises that He will fulfill the desire of the one who fears Him.

And Psalm 37:4 tells us that God will give us the desires of our hearts if we delight in Him.

Yes, the biblical writers were not afraid of chasing and embracing their dreams. They knew that God wants to make our deepest dreams come true. And that He Himself is the key that turns the lock on the most wonderful of our dreams.

My long struggle with depression began to dissipate when I stopped apologizing for not being what others expected of me, and instead pursued with unbridled passion the call that God had put within me.

Perfect love casts out fear, and my fears of failure had to find the nearest exit.

So, get rid of fear. Show it the door.

Embrace hope.

Chase it. Track it down. Then bathe in it.

Do not proceed with caution.

Don't die with your song unsung.

44

THE (ANTI) SUICIDE SQUAD

I get lots of texts and messages and emails from people who tell me that they really just want to die. Some of them are cutters. Some of them are overcome by guilt. Some of them feel like they have no value to anybody.

Like they are just goo on a cosmic shoe.

And when people feel like this, they don't feel like they have the energy to go on.

I'm not going to tell you that life isn't hard sometimes. But I am going to tell you that God has a special place in His heart for those who feel broken, to whom life has dealt a bad hand, or who are struggling just to keep their head above the water. He cares about the hurting heart.

Psalm 56 tells us that God collects all your tears in a bottle. That is how much your pain matters to Him.

In Old Testament times, women would often collect their tears and keep them in special tear bottles. Whether the tears were happy or sad, they were deemed too precious to be wasted. The tears spoke of a woman's times of deepest sadness or her most extraordinary gladness, of uncontrolled giddy glee and the most heartrending grief. Then, when the day came, she would give this bottle of tears to the man she married. How terribly romantic.

Might want to keep that in mind for Valentine's Day, huh?

I know of one great Bible scholar (who just happens to be, *ahem*, my dad) who suggests that in the story in the Gospels where the prostitute washed Jesus' feet with her tears and then dried them with her hair, that she probably did this by emptying her tear bottle in an act of tender devotion. She was, in a sense, declaring herself a bride of Christ. Beautiful thought, isn't it?

Tears are often more eloquent than words can ever be.

Tears can be the most powerful of prayers.

(((())))

Your tears matter to God because you matter to God.

He knows the brokenness in your heart. None of your pain has gone unnoticed.

The Bible contains about 900 references to the heart, and when the heart speaks, it isn't just referring to the tough little muscle that pumps your blood. It speaks of the sum and seat and center of who you are— the nexus of your emotional existence. And the idea of the broken heart? It can be traced all the way back to ancient Hebrew literature. In fact, the Bible invented the phrase "a broken heart"!

God wants to heal your broken heart.

And at the same time He wants to use your brokenness to heal others.

The scars you share with others can become lighthouses to warn those headed toward the same rocks that nearly shipwrecked you.

◯◯◯◯

The storms can't take us to a place where God can't keep us. Jesus slept right through a raging storm out on the sea while the waves buffeted the boat with their fierce turbulence. But when the disciples cried out in fear, Jesus awoke immediately. The wind and the waves could not wake Him, but the cry of human need could.

It still can.

◯◯◯◯

A woman came up to me after a recent talk and shared that she had been seriously considering suicide, but that the words of hope I offered had made her rethink how much her life meant. She found hope in the words of hope I was sharing. Certainly not hope based upon me, but hope based upon God's love and promises for her.

I just listened to her story while my eyes pooled with tears.

◯◯◯◯

And here's the thing. Even if you don't feel like you can muster enough hope to go on—that isn't a problem. Because we not only have God, we have each other. We can hold each other up through the tough times, and offer strength, encouragement, and caring when the path ahead seems too hard to travel.

I call my daily radio program "Hope Generation" because it is about a pun that offers both a personal and a collective appeal:

First, we are building a generation of hope globally.

Second, we can produce hope generation in each heart individually (generation can also mean creation). We create holy happiness and change this planet by dealing out hope galore.

In my struggles with depression over the years, it was always my friends who managed to help pull me out of the despair. I learned that I couldn't go it alone, and that I was never meant to.

My friends didn't help me by offering valuable therapeutic insights or some sort of complex intervention. They didn't try to talk me out of my pain and depression. The way they healed my heartbreak was by grabbing a longboard and skating with me…without a single word about the grief I'd been through.

Their optimism, their fun, their craziness, their love…those are the things that put my broken heart back together again and reminded me that I mattered. That we all do.

Jean Paul Sartre famously believed that "hell is other people."

That's probably because he never had a chance to hang with the Optimisfits.

45

IMPOSSIBLE IS NOT
IN MY DICTIONARY

"Impossible" is a word found only in the dictionary of fools. With God, nothing is impossible. No heartbreak is too large to be healed. No disappointment too deep to be overcome. No failure too horrible to be forgiven.

Impossible, to an Optimisfit, is more of a dare than a declaration.

We follow the God who is Lord of the Impossible.

⦅⦆

So, don't trust your eyes. Salt looks just like sugar. When your eyes deceive you, and tell you that God isn't there or that He has forgotten you, don't believe it for a minute. When it looks like your circumstances are most dire, is when you must remember that we walk by faith, not by sight.

Faithcast: One hundred percent chance of winning.

Just because the storm is present, doesn't mean that our Savior is absent. Eleanor Roosevelt once said, "You gain strength, courage, and confidence by every experience in which you really look fear in the face. You must do the thing which you think you cannot do."

Optimisfits aren't scared of death, so why should we fear anything on this side of death?

⸭

Worry is absurd. The famous mathematician Kurt Gödel worried himself sick. He was terrified of being poisoned, so he wouldn't eat any food that had not been prepared by his wife. When she got sick and was hospitalized, he literally starved to death. Surely, he knew that his fear of being poisoned was less credible than the reality of starvation, but he couldn't bring himself to eat. He starved to death at the age of 71.

Like Gödel, it is often our imagined fears that do more damage than anything based on reality. We are so worried about everything that the fear itself kills us in the end.

⸭

In his book *The Artisan Soul*, Erwin McManus writes:

> Sometimes life comes with such blunt force trauma that the natural and human response is to curl up in a fetal position and hope that somehow the world will just go away. Yet incredibly we soon meet someone else who has suffered just as deeply and yet that person has somehow risen above their pain. They remember the pain but are no longer trapped in it. Occasionally we have the privilege of meeting that rare individual whose story is filled with such overwhelming tragedy that we wonder how in the world they can see so much beauty all around them. Yet those people do exist—people who have suffered more than you or me and yet remain more hopeful, more optimistic, and yes, even more joyful and happy.[8]

⬭⬭⬭

I was recently asked on a TV interview if I considered myself an introvert or an extrovert. I thought about it for a moment and said that such distinctions were too binary for my taste. So right there and then we came up with a new personality type that described me: the *Godfident hopetrovert*. Using that phrase may make your spell check go into spasms, but it seems exactly right to me.

If you've been an Optimisfit for any time at all you know that on your worst day with God you are better off than on your best day without God. Because when you're going through your worst, God is busy planning His best.

There are plenty of people reminding us that we are all going to die soon. We need some people to remind us that we ain't dead yet.

There are plenty of people who want to "tell it like it is." But the world needs some more people who tell it like it *can* be.

There is no room in our dictionary for *impossible*.

46

THERE'S A LION IN TOWN

Solomon didn't acquire gold as plentiful as stones by just sitting around.

He worked hard to achieve all he achieved, so in his book, "lazy" was a bad word. Throughout the pages of Proverbs, he mercilessly roasts lazy people. Over and over again, he talks about how laziness keeps us from living a good life.

My favorite example is Proverbs 26:13 when he quotes the lazy man as saying, "There is a lion in the streets." That's his reason for inaction. Now, think about it. A lion can run up to 35 miles per hour and jump 30 feet in a single bound. It is a scary beast, and one that would, without blinking, be happy to make a Manwich out of you. The lion is a frightening critter. But here's the thing, you were never going to find a lion roaming in the streets of a Jewish town in Solomon's day. And you certainly wouldn't today.

A lazy person is someone who specializes in making excuses. And when they can't find a legitimate one, an imaginary one will do.

Like that lion down on Third and Main.

The Book of Ecclesiastes warns that if you are always waiting for the perfect working conditions to arrive, you'll never get anything done.

Jesus never had good working conditions. He was always beset by harsh critics, religious zealots, and curious onlookers who just wanted to see another miracle. And in the end, His most faithful followers proved less than dependable.

He was misunderstood, falsely accused, and then betrayed.

But through it all He kept to His mission. Because He knew that mission had come from God.

Jesus worked hard. Right before He died, He prayed, "I have finished the work You have given Me to do" (John 17:4 NKJV).

He was committed to the task He'd been given, and He gave His all. Literally gave His all. And the result was that He single-handedly built a kingdom.

Napoleon Bonaparte once said, "I know men, and I tell you that Jesus Christ is no mere man. Alexander, Caesar, Charlemagne, and I have founded empires. But on what did we rest the creation of our genius? Upon force. Jesus Christ founded His empire upon love; and at this hour millions of men would die for Him."

Jesus was crucified with a sign above His cross that read: "King of the Jews." This title was written in Latin, Greek, and Hebrew—and there is a reason for that. Latin was the language of the Roman Empire: politics. Greek was the language of the great thinkers like Socrates, Plato, and Aristotle: philosophy. And Hebrew was the language of the Old Testament: religion. The Gospel writer was showing us that Jesus was the King of all three realms. This is just a gentle assertion of low-key world domination!

⬤⬤⬤⬤

The best leaders are driven.

Napoleon built an empire that stretched from Spain to Poland because he was willing to work for it. He was single-minded in his focus. When he would attend the opera he usually looked bored, but it was really because he was busy plotting in his mind about how he could combine the three army corps at Frankfurt with the two in Cologne. He never shut off his brain and he kept it focused.

Julius Caesar was no less driven. When he had leisure time in Spain, he used it to read a book about Alexander the Great. His companions noticed the tears in his eyes as he was reading and asked him what was wrong. Caesar replied, "Do you not think it is a matter for sorrow that while Alexander, at my age was already king of so many peoples, I have as yet achieved no such brilliant success?"

Alexander braved deserts and mountains, and took his troops to places no one else would dare to go. He didn't even fear the elephants of Hannibal, whose tusks were sometimes sharpened and laced with poison. When Alexander's men wanted to turn back from India, he did everything in his power to keep them from turning back so he could continue his world conquest. He bid them to soldier on. One time when he was parched in the middle of a desert with no water anywhere to be found, he was offered a leftover bit of water in a helmet, which he refused to drink. He didn't want to quench his own thirst when none of his men could do likewise. He knew how to motivate his troops, and because of that he conquered the known world by the time he was 32.

No wonder Julius Caesar felt he couldn't measure up.

In reality these were all just people like you and me.

With one key difference—they were focused and driven.

If we can harness that kind of focus and drive, what is to prevent us Optimisfits from conquering the world?

〇〇〇〇〇

Some of my friends ask me how I can stand living out of a suitcase as I travel around the world giving ten speeches a week, or how I can memorize the long sermons I deliver without notes, or how I can get by on a minimal amount of sleep while I am doing that. My secret is this: I am focused and driven. It's not even a question about the *how*. My *why* is stronger than my *how*.

Why am I willing to work hard to get out my message? Because this planet is sinking into hopelessness and I refuse to accept that.

I want to help rewrite that narrative.

Me and my Squad—and you, dear reader—we need to be about change.

That is my *why*. The *how* is all in the details about working hard.

〇〇〇〇〇

Who wouldn't want to dance like Michael Jackson?

But how many people would be willing to lock themselves in a room every Sunday and practice the entire day like he did, month after month and year after year?

Who wouldn't want to experience the excitement of being a Navy Seal?

But how many people want to undergo 96 hours of sleep deprivation and hypothermia and all kinds of indignities as part of the training during "hell week"?

Who wouldn't want to be David, lopping off the head of mighty Goliath?

But how many people are willing to take on lions and bears as part of the preparation for battle against the enemy giant?

If we want to change the world, we have to be willing to work for it.

In wartime, Churchill told the people of Britain that he could only offer them blood, sweat, toil, and tears…but that it would be worth it in the end. That is what I would say to any Optimisfit who wants to make a difference in this world.

It won't always be easy.

But it will be worth it.

If we want to share in His glory, we must share in His suffering.

Our dreams might be beautiful things, but we can't leave them on the pillow. We must drag them out into our reality. Sir Robert Scott, the great Arctic explorer, was once described as being "a strange mixture of the dreamy and the practical, and never more practical than immediately after he'd been dreamy." This is the killer combo that unleashes greatness: dreamy practicality.

When you combine big dreams with hard work you have the key to making things happen. If you aren't working hard it's because you aren't believing in the power of your dreams.

Inspiration is always the result of perspiration. It's the vision that keeps us going strong.

Dreamy practicality.

If your dad tells you that you must clean out the family car, you probably won't put in too much effort. You'll quickly wipe off some of the dust on the dashboard, and run a vacuum over the floor mats, and then you'll call it good. You do just enough to keep him from getting mad at you.

If, on the other hand, Dad has given you the keys to the family car so you can use it on your date with that girl you have a ginormous crush on, you'll make sure every surface is totally clean, then you'll bust out the Turtle Wax for extra shine. You'll wipe down all the windows and polish up the chrome wheels, and you'll even hang one of those little trees on the rearview mirror to cover any stray odors. You get it all tricked out, and you'll have fun doing it.

No one forces you to do it, you do it because you are compelled by love.

That my friends, is the difference between operating in Law and operating in Love. Love will always take you further than Law. Especially when you are crushing on the God of hope.

And the result of such passion is excellence. When you aren't trying it is because you aren't caring. When you do what you love, nobody will have to get on your case. You'll work harder because you are motivated.

So, locate your dream.

And pursue it fiercely.

〇〇〇〇〇

There *is* a lion in town.

The Lion of Judah.

What's your excuse?

47

HOPE DEALERS

You got problems? Yeah, well, welcome to humanity. Just last weekend I spoke in Cincinnati and some guy protested the event with a hand-lettered sign and contacted the local news station to spread lies about me and my family. Life can be hard sometimes.

In the immortal words of Kurt Vonnegut: "So it goes."

But how you deal with the hard stuff depends on your perspective.

Let's consider Job for a moment, the legend from the Old Testament whose name has become synonymous with suffering. Job, we tend to think, was the guy who drew the short straw. Most modern-day Christians think that Job's life was horrible. But maybe that is because we aren't looking at the full picture.

Most biblical scholars agree that the events recorded in the book of Job took place over about a nine-month period. Think about that for a minute. The sufferings of Job were intense, for sure. Really bad. But they lasted less than a year. Then, according to the biblical account, Job went on to live for 140 more years after this time of suffering had ended.

That's 140 years.

And, when it was all said and done, he ended up with twice as much as he had before. Twice the cattle, twice the sheep, twice the wealth, twice the joy, and even twice the kids.

When you think about it, his biggest loss had been his kids, but he gained the exact same number of new children as those he had lost in the catastrophe. In the long run he had twice as many kids as before, though half of them had now changed addresses. They were in Paradise.

So, on the other side of the struggle, Job had twice as much as before. The promise of Zechariah had proven true: "Return to your fortress, you prisoners of hope, even now I announce that I will restore twice as much to you" (Zechariah 9:12 NIV).

Job seemed to have lost everything—health, wealth, family, reputation. But in the long run he would be okay. He should have chosen to relax and *sit back*, because every *setback* is a *setup* for a *comeback*! In the long run, he ended up having the best life he could imagine.

The nine months were an interim period. And such periods are probably inevitable for all of us. The nine months were the labor pangs before he gave birth to a brighter tomorrow.

Ask any mom if it was worth the nine months of discomfort to give birth to her child. No mom ever looks at her baby and says, "Well, *that* wasn't worth it."

Nine months of intense suffering was nothing when compared to the 140 years of intense joy that followed.

So, don't judge your life by this moment right now. Don't think the script of the present season of your life sets the tone for everything that follows. You have a brighter future on the other side of your own Job-like time of struggle.

God is leading His children from gory to glory. Victory is already determined in the final act. So, hold on during the hard times. Relax. Trust God. Look ahead.

No matter how badly you might think you are losing right now, there is no reason to be hopeless. You might think that you've lost the plot, but the Author of your story knows what is coming next. And that our story is a love story, a story of healing, a story of hope, and a story of ultimate victory.

Our hope, our joy, our happiness—these things are not based upon our current circumstances.

Our best days are still in front of us.

Does that seem overly optimistic? Well, we aren't called Optimisfits for no reason.

Is the glass half full? Is the glass half empty? No, if you look at the bigger picture, then the cup is overflowing.

If we've already won the game—and we have through the God of hope—then all that's left is to celebrate and have fun. We are Gryffindor. We will beat Slytherin every time. The snake has been crushed, and we are the winners. We are just mopping up after the victory and turning the page on our pains.

We may suffer for a little while, but something better is ahead.

That's why Optimisfits are hope dealers.

∞∞∞

What a difference a year makes.

A couple of years ago I arrived at a resort in Palm Springs all by myself and full of heartbreak. I spent a week soaking in the pain while I soaked in the sun. I walked around the resort empty, lonely, and confused about my future. So much of what I had dreamed life would be like had now become just a memory mocking my present misery.

This year I returned with my some of my Squad—Cambria, Bo, and Brighton. Life seemed so different now than it did during that dark year of my life. We vlogged while we splashed in the gurgling muddy hot springs, we explored caves as though we were Navy Seals on a mission. We took selfies in front of a vibey neon palm tree, and snuck onto a waterslide at midnight at an upscale resort. We skateboarded through a forest of lights and danced to '80s music. We laughed until we cried.

There was a time when I wondered if I could ever be truly happy again, and here I was taking hold of happiness with both hands. God used my friends to redeem the bad memories and rewrite that chapter of life with a Magic Marker called…

Hope.

48

HORNS AND RED TIGHTS?

Throughout this book I have been talking about the supernatural enemy we face in our day-to-day battles of life. He's the one we call the devil, or Satan.

Now let's clear up a couple things about the original "Dark Lord."

First, he is the source of the bad stuff that happens to us, not God. I often hear Christians say, "The Lord gives and the Lord takes away. Blessed be the name of the Lord." Yes, that is in the Bible. Job 1:21 to be exact. But pay attention to this fact. God didn't say this. Job said it.

Frankly, during his time of struggle Job said a lot of things that weren't really true. By the end of the book of Job, God has to straighten out his bad theology.

If you are actually paying attention to what you are reading, you'll note right away that it was Satan who took away what God had given to Job.

Who took Job's kids? Satan.

Who took Job's health? Satan.

Who took Job's possessions? Satan.

See a pattern emerging?

Please don't attribute to God the work of the enemy.

And at the end of the story, who is it that restores these things to Job? Yep. God. And He restored them double. Although Job's trouble doubled, in the end God gave him double for his trouble! God is not the One who takes away. He is the One who gives. Blessed be His name.

At the beginning of Job's story, it was a stormy whirlwind that killed his kids. Then at the end of the story, it is through the whirlwind that God speaks to Job. The place where we suffer most painfully is often the place where God speaks most powerfully.

⫘

Second, let's be clear that the devil isn't a sunburned faun with cleft hooves and horns and red tights, who twirls his mustache ominously and zaps people with his trident. This cartoon version of our Great Adversary only leads us to question his reality.

You'll find a better picture by reflecting on J.R.R. Tolkien's creation story in *The Silmarillion*. When the Eldar sing Middle Earth into existence, there is a fallen angel (Morgoth) who adds discordant notes to this heavenly music to misshape the new creation. Then, his servant Sauron becomes the source of the evil that is troubling Middle Earth in *The Lord of the Rings*. His malign presence is there throughout the tale, trying to destroy all that is good and beautiful in the world of Elves, Dwarves, and humans. The whole story is an epic battle of good versus evil that parallels the story of our world.

Life is a battle.

We are in hand-to-hand combat with a powerful foe. But he is a foe who has already been defeated by the God of hope.

Psalm 37 tells us that God laughs when the enemy plots how to destroy His kids.

The Lord laughs because He knows he's betting on a fixed fight!

49

HEARTBREAK AND HOPE

I've been through a lot of heartbreak in my short lifetime. My sister died in her VW Bug. My brother fought a long, raging battle against brain tumors that nearly brought about his exit from the planet. I got so heartbroken about a romantic relationship that I actually thought the suffering might kill me. It was pain beyond pain. And I've done battle with severe depression and at one particularly low moment even seriously considered the option of suicide.

Once, I even took up a knife to end the pain. But I thought about what Sylvia Plath wrote in *The Bell Jar* about the time she was planning to slash her wrists and this thought ran through her mind:

> But when it came right down to it, the skin on my wrist looked so white and defenseless that I couldn't do it. It was as if what I wanted to kill wasn't in that skin or the thin blue pulse that jumped under my thumb, but somewhere else, deeper, more secret, and a whole lot harder to get at.[9]

Like Plath, my life has provided enough material for years of nightmares.

But I have dreams. And these have proven more powerful than my nightmares. In fact, my nightmares have prepared me for my dreams.

Your pain is in service to your destiny. As my favorite novelist, Matthew Stover, has written: "Pain either has the power to break you, or it is the power that makes you unbreakable. What it is depends on who you are."

(((()))

Sometimes clichés are true.

What doesn't kill you makes you stronger.

Tears make you braver.

Heartbreak makes you wiser.

That's why pain doesn't scare me so much anymore. When you've lived through some nightmares, but kept going farther up and further in, up and to the right…you start to lose your fear of the White Witch. She may try to turn you into a statue of ice, brittle and on the point of shattering, but the warm breath of Aslan will begin to thaw you out, and empower you to defeat her. You'll find yourself alive, awake, and ready to fight back.

One day you'll thank your past for creating a better future.

Outlook determines outcome, so when the outlook is bleak, try the *up*look. Get a different perspective. The problem is never just the problem; the problem is my perception of the problem. When the problem is too big for me, then it is just the right size for God.

(((()))

I know depression. As the poet said, "I myself am hell; nobody's there." But don't feel sorry for me. You've experienced the darkness too.

And when you take the long view of things, you find that it brings things into proper perspective. What may seem like a big deal may not be such a big deal in the big picture.

The universe moves forward, and so shall I. I'm not going to waste a lot of time looking back at the pain I've been through, lest I veer off my course. I'm racing toward the great Unknown, which is the place where God will fully make Himself known. I'm banking everything on the God who is with me on this journey for that day when I drink the milk of paradise.

But I don't want to tell you that it will always be easy.

Because that would be a lie.

⟨⟨⟨⟩⟩⟩

Depression has dogged my steps. And sometimes it felt like it was going to do me in.

Sometimes all I could do was sit and stare at the wall, wondering what might be the best way to do myself in. And I knew I was at my darkest moment when I began to feel nothing. I got to the point where I felt no emotion at all. Just an emotional flatline.

And my heart felt dead as stone.

But as alienated as I felt, I was not left an orphan. It may have felt that way for a while, but it wasn't true.

When you are a child of God you are never alone. Never, ever. You will never be less lonely than when you get alone with God.

My God was *Abba*, which is a highly personal word in the Aramaic language of Jesus. And it was the word with which He addressed God.

When you think back to how the surrounding cultures thought about their gods, you realize how revolutionary it was to call God *Abba*, which effectively means *Daddy*. No Greek would ever have thought of referring to Zeus as their caring papa, nor would any Roman talk about Jupiter in that way. To them, God was frightening, often angry, and always unpredictable. The ancient gods were not good material for caring fathers. So, when Jesus and Paul told the Jews and the Greeks that God was *Abba*, that was about as subversive and iconoclastic as it was possible to be. It introduced an unheard-of sort of intimacy into how people thought about the Source, the Universe, God.

Daddy. What kind of image does that conjure up in your mind? Hopefully you were raised with a daddy who loved you, cared for you, and loved to hold you in his lap and tell you how much he adored you. That is the picture of God's love that Abba implies. And if you didn't have an earthly father who lavished such care upon you, it is wonderful to know that now you have just such a Heavenly Daddy. You are besties with God. You are chill with the Almighty.

So many people ask me, "How can I get closer to God?"

My answer is, "You can't. God is inside you, so how can you get any closer than that?" You just need to let Him love you.

Jesus came to help us see and experience what God's love looked like. And He was tortured and killed, and He suffered because of His love for humanity. He knows what suffering feels like. He can fully sympathize with all the hurt and pain and confusion and loneliness and rejection we feel.

The book of Hebrews tells us that Jesus is our High Priest. In the Old Testament the high priest spoke to God for the people and spoke to the people for God. But Jesus was more than just our representative. He was the sacrifice itself. He gave Himself so that He could fully sympathize with all our struggles. He became one of us so that our tears would be joined to the tears of God.

He puts all His weight behind me, and He uses the things meant to wound me to make me strong.

The Mighty God who fights our battles alongside us is the God who invites us into His lap of love, where He whispers *sweet everythings* into our ears.

Psalm 23 ("The Lord is my Shepherd") is one of the most popular passages in the whole Bible. I love the fact that it was written by someone who'd grown up learning the art of being a shepherd himself. He had worked to corral the straying sheep, faced down the wolves and other snarling predators, and spent long nights making sure that his lambs were safe even when it was too dark to see.

David wrote of walking through the valley of the shadow of death—and that is probably a valley where we have all spent some time—but in the midst of that darkness, he sings that he "fears no evil." Why? Because God is with him.

Every step of the way.

The valley couldn't be avoided. He didn't lie down in the valley. He didn't stop and set up his tent there. He couldn't circumnavigate it. He. Just. Kept. Walking.

One step at a time. Through the valley.

Churchill is reported to have said, "If you're going through hell, keep going."

Don't stay in the place of despair. Keep following the Shepherd who will lead you through.

We can't control what happens to us, but we can control what happens through us. Let's just keep moving. There is a battle to be won.

There is an enemy who needs a good judo kick in the trachea.

There is a dark world that needs the light.

⬤⬤⬤⬤

Sometimes it is an ugly world.

Apartheid. Racism. Genocide. Rape. Murder. Bullying. Greed. Cheating. Vicious gossip. Sweatshops. Poverty. Unfair trade. Sexism. War. Terrorism. Torture. Lies.

And that is just Tuesday.

But in Philippians 2:15, Paul tells us that we shine as lights in a wicked and perverse generation. The word he uses for lights is *phosteres*, which is the same word that the Septuagint uses in its translation of Genesis 1, where we are told that God puts the great lights in space. In other words, the same word that is being used in the description from the creation story of the heavenly lamps in space is being used for those who are God's children. The darker the night on earth, the easier to see the stars in the heavens above. So against the backdrop of the darkness of the world, we are *phosteres*. The dark is just a backdrop against which we shine all the brighter!

The darker the heavens are, the more clearly we can look up to the heavens and watch the stars shine.

Steph Curry is a basketball star. Selena Gomez is a pop star. But you and me? We can be Kingdom stars! In fact, Daniel 12:3 says that those who are wise will shine like stars eternally.

You may not feel much like a star. The darkness may seem so overpowering to you that you feel on the verge of collapse. But remember...

For a star to be born, there is one thing that must happen. A gaseous nebula must collapse. So go ahead and collapse. This is not your destruction. This is your birth.

God is forging you into a star.

50

TAKE THE RED PILL

I've already told you that Cam doesn't watch movies. He lives them. Then he makes his own.

So, you can imagine my surprise when my phone started to go ballistic a few nights ago. He texted to tell me that he had just—finally— watched *The Matrix*. *Well, it's about time* was my first thought. But once he started to enthuse about it, it didn't so much seem like he had watched it as that he had been slain in the Spirit by it. It positively leveled him.

Cameron swallowed the red pill and then he blew up my phone with about a billion texts, give or take a few. He had seen a new vision. He was Neo and he wasn't even kidding. It may have taken him 20 years to finally watch the movie, but it was a fresh and fierce revelation for him.

Delirium ensued.

Cam: "My brain got baptized! I'm going ballistic! I just realized that we live in the freaking Matrix! We are in the Matrix! This is all a joke! This world is not even real. It is all a figment of our brain! This is all a freaking illusion. Everything we know is a lie. The world is ours! The WHOLE WORLD! WE CAN DO ANYTHING! I literally came out of that movie believing that I can do everything. And I can't be convinced otherwise."

Then he texted (and I quote): "AHDJSNXJANNXJD"

Your guess is as good as mine.

I messaged him back: "You better believe these texts are going in my book."

Cam: "YOU BETTER BECAUSE THIS IS WHAT'S GOING TO SAVE THE WORLD!"

Cam: "Actually, forget writing a book. We are writing history."

◯◯◯◯◯

Cameron knows that his kind either end up in the White House or the Nut House. He is no common Muggle. He sees things that most normal mortals don't see. Who knows? He might actually *be* a fresh incarnation of Neo.

What he knows is that he doesn't have to live a normal life. He thinks a normal life is great and all that, and it is super dope except for the one small problem: Normal life is for chumps.

Other than that, he's all for it.

Cam is convinced that he can heal diseases. He thinks he can levitate spoons. He believes he will live to be 900 years old. And that's lowballing it.

When Jesus said that we will never die, he takes that quite literally.

Many of history's most accomplished people walked the edge of sanity.

Patton thought he was a Viking in a previous life. He thought he had fought Caesar. Ernest Hemingway put on a tough macho persona. Probably because his mother insisted on dressing him up like a little girl when he was a child. Billy Sunday shadowboxed with the devil. Luther threw an inkpot at the devil. To this day you can see the stain on the wall of the castle where he was staying when he had a visit from the Prince of Darkness.

Normal, boring, sane people generally don't change the world.

Well-adjusted people don't generally rewrite the rules of existence.

So, maybe Cameron, the neo-Neo, might just have a point. If Cam is nuts, well, I wouldn't have him any other way. This giant ball of water and dirt, which is hurtling through space at 67,000 miles per hour, has a history of being course corrected by humans who might well have been diagnosed as mad. So, go ahead. Embrace your inner crazy.

(XXX)

There was a time when I wanted to die. And that is true for many members of my Squad. We never felt like we really fit in. That we couldn't live up to the expectations of all the people who pretended to have everything all figured out. And the world they had figured out for us was a boring, vanilla, death-dealing, and hopeless place. Life seemed like a drawn-out death sentence.

So, we said no.

And then we decided to quit listening to the naysayers, the conformity-mongers, and the dream-killers.

We decided that if we were going to grind, we were going to grind on behalf of our dreams. We were going to embrace the adventure and enjoy our lives. We were going to have fun. We were going to chase the things that mattered. We were going to bring heaven to earth. We were going to have a great time doing it.

We were…and are…going to do things differently.

Who ever heard of writing a whole book on your iPhone? Guess what? I just did.

◯◯◯◯

There will probably be some professional Pharisees who find this way of thinking to be unsafe, unsound, or even heretical. They might accuse me of being antinomian. (You can look that up if you really want, but honestly, I'm not.) They can blog their displeasure and argue that I am off-base.

Whatever.

I think I'll just grab my board and play some EDM while I go bombing down the street.

I think I'll say no to the ordinary, the conformist, and the normal—and I'll stretch my imagination toward a different way of thinking and feeling and experiencing life.

I think I'll let myself get lost in the wonder.

I think I'll prove that fun is fundamental.

I think I'll say no to the System, and its offer of being a cog in its gears.

I think I'll nourish my inner rebel.

I think I'll proudly wear the lapel of a *hope dealer*.

So, let's raise our communion glasses and give a high-five to the universe, because we are about to show a hopeless world what it means to be invaded by…

The Optimisfits.

NOTES

Chapter 8—Ugly Paul and Monster Barbie

1. Galia Slayen, "The Scary Reality of a Real-Life Barbie Doll," *Huffington Post*, April 8, 2011, https://www.huffingtonpost.com/entry/the-scary-reality-of-a-re_b_845239.html.

Chapter 11—The Wardrobe Effect

2. G.K. Chesterton, *Orthodoxy* (New York: John Lane Company, 1909), 108-09.

Chapter 19—Walt Disney Has No Good Ideas

3. Simon Paige, *The Very Best of Winston Churchill* (Createspace Independent Publisher, 2014).

4. Mel Robbins, *The 5 Second Rule* (Dallas: The Savio Republic, 2017).

5. Taiwo Odukoya, *Limitless* (Lagos, Nigeria: Grace Springs Africa Publishers, 2007), 60.

Chapter 26—What Sherlock Holmes Taught Me About My Attic

6. Sir Arthur Conan Doyle, *A Study in Scarlet* (London: Ward, Lock, Bowden, and Co., 1892), 20.

Chapter 30—The Unedited Me

7. Quotes.net, STANDS4 LLC, 2018, *"Ralph Waldo Emerson Quotes."* Accessed July 20, 2018. https://www.quotes.net/quote/44572.

Chapter 45—Impossible Is Not in My Dictionary

8. Erwin McManus, *The Artisan Soul* (New York: HarperCollins, 2014), 83.

Chapter 49—Heartbreak and Hope

9. Sylvia Plath, *The Bell Jar* (New York: Harper & Row, 1971), 121.

ACKNOWLEDGMENTS

So yeah, this is all Terry Glaspey's fault. If it weren't for him, this book wouldn't be in your hands. I didn't have an agent, nor was I looking for a book deal when Terry discovered me and proposed publishing this project. On finding out that he edited one of my all-time favorite authors, I was a goner. There's no word wizard I'd rather work with. His literary prowess has turned my stream-of-consciousness style into a coherent flow, and his editorial process is a fearsome and wondrous thing to behold. It was a joy working with this legend.

I'm also possessed of a gratitude attitude when I think of Shannon Hartley, Sherrie Slopianka, Bob Hawkins, Jessica Bellastrazze, and all the wonderful people at Harvest House. Their belief in and enthusiasm for *Optimisfits* was germane and integral to its realization.

I am wildly thankful for the Hope Gen team: John Swenson, Jereme Dittmer, and the Bates boys: Jeff, Taylor, and Dylan. Their book trailers, radio spots, creative ideas and ideals, along with their unflagging support, provided marketing musculature for *Optimisfits* even when it was just a poor skeleton.

I want to thank my sister Christy for her vision-casting and muse-singing when it comes to the bold élan of wrestling a book to the ground, and her husband, Seth, for coming up with the title *Optimisfits*. My other brothers and sisters, Mary, Shea, Peter, and Amanda, as well as my dad, offered tons of encouragement nourishment! And lastly, I want to thank my mom. When depression went all Apple-rainbow death-wheel on me and I seized up, she brought me back to life. When I thought the world had buried me, she reminded me I was a seed.

ABOUT THE AUTHOR

Ben Courson is the founder of Hope Generation, has a global TV and radio program, and is a gifted and nationally renowned speaker. His humorous, uplifting, and high-energy style couples with a gift to communicate God's heart in an impactful way. His ultimate mission is to generate hope in God to build a generation of hope in others.

bencourson.com

WE HOPE YOU ENJOYED
OPTIMISFITS

Hope Generation and Ben Courson have many ways for you to enjoy their content. As you do, you'll find yourself being encouraged in the deepest part of your being and you will also become a "Hope Dealer," making a beautiful impact in your sphere of the world. Follow us on…

BENCOURSON.COM

HILLSONG CHANNEL

HOPE GENERATION APP

HOPE GENERATION PODCAST

"We have this hope as an anchor for the soul…"
— Hebrews 6:19 (NIV)